FAMILIES AND FREEDOM

FAMILIES

AND

FREEDOM

A

Documentary History

OF

AFRICAN-AMERICAN KINSHIP

IN

THE CIVIL WAR ERA

EDITED BY

IRA BERLIN AND LESLIE S. ROWLAND

MCMXCVII.

THE NEW PRESS · NEW YORK

OTHER PUBLICATIONS OF
THE FREEDMEN AND SOUTHERN SOCIETY PROJECT

Freedom: A Documentary History of Emancipation, 1861–1867

Series 1, volume 1, *The Destruction of Slavery*, ed. Ira Berlin, Barbara J. Fields, Thavolia Glymph, Joseph P. Reidy, and Leslie S. Rowland (1985)

Series 1, volume 2, *The Wartime Genesis of Free Labor: The Upper South*, ed. Ira Berlin, Steven F. Miller, Joseph P. Reidy, and Leslie S. Rowland (1993)

Series 1, volume 3, *The Wartime Genesis of Free Labor: The Lower South*, ed. Ira Berlin, Thavolia Glymph, Steven F. Miller, Joseph P. Reidy, Leslie S. Rowland, and Julie Saville (1990)

Series 2, *The Black Military Experience*, ed. Ira Berlin, Joseph P. Reidy, and Leslie S. Rowland (1982)

Free at Last: A Documentary History of Slavery, Freedom, and the Civil War, ed. Ira Berlin, Barbara J. Fields, Steven F. Miller, Joseph P. Reidy, and Leslie S. Rowland (1992)

Slaves No More: Three Essays on Emancipation and the Civil War, by Ira Berlin, Barbara J. Fields, Steven F. Miller, Joseph P. Reidy, and Leslie S. Rowland (1992)

LIBRARY OF CONGRESS CATALOGING-IN-PUBLICATION DATA

Families and freedom: a documentary history of African-American kinship in the Civil War era /
edited by Ira Berlin and Leslie S. Rowland.
p.   cm.
Includes bibliographical references and index.
ISBN 1-56584-026-7
1. Freedmen—Correspondence. 2. Afro-American families—History—19th century—Sources.
3. Slaves—Emancipation—United States—Sources.
4. Afro-Americans—History—1863-1877—Sources. I. Berlin, Ira. II. Rowland, Leslie S.
E185.2.F27   1997
973'.0496073—dc20
96-24826   CIP

PUBLISHED IN THE UNITED STATES BY THE NEW PRESS, NEW YORK
DISTRIBUTED BY W.W. NORTON & COMPANY, INC., NEW YORK

ESTABLISHED IN 1990 AS A MAJOR ALTERNATIVE TO THE LARGE COMMERCIAL PUBLISHING HOUSES, THE NEW PRESS IS A FULL-SCALE, NONPROFIT AMERICAN BOOK PUBLISHER OUTSIDE OF THE UNIVERSITY PRESSES. THE PRESS IS OPERATED EDITORIALLY IN THE PUBLIC INTEREST, RATHER THAN FOR PRIVATE GAIN; IT IS COMMITTED TO PUBLISHING, IN INNOVATIVE WAYS, WORKS OF EDUCATIONAL, CULTURAL, AND COMMUNITY VALUE THAT, DESPITE THEIR INTELLECTUAL MERITS, MIGHT NOT NORMALLY BE COMMERCIALLY VIABLE. THE NEW PRESS'S EDITORIAL OFFICES ARE LOCATED AT
THE CITY UNIVERSITY OF NEW YORK.

BOOK DESIGN BY CHARLES NIX

PRINTED IN THE UNITED STATES OF AMERICA

9 8 7 6 5 4 3 2 1

CONTENTS

ACKNOWLEDGMENTS

Families and Freedom rests upon two decades of collective labor by the editors of the Freedmen and Southern Society Project. The historians with whom we have constructed the project's archives, established its editorial standards, and edited the volumes of *Freedom: A Documentary History of Emancipation* have provided both scholarly foundation and collegial inspiration for *Families and Freedom*. We hope this volume does justice to their legacy.

Leaning upon the work of the Freedmen and Southern Society Project also makes us liable for its debts. These too we are pleased to acknowledge. The College of Arts and Humanities of the University of Maryland has been a warm supporter of the project from its inception. So have the nation's two major funders of historical documentary editions, the National Historical Publications and Records Commission and the National Endowment for the Humanities. Both have come under siege of late, often by those who insist that there is no such thing as a "free lunch" while supping freely at history's table. We hope that *Families and Freedom* suggests some of the ways in which investment in basic research in the humanities helps to make for an informed public—no small matter in a constitutional democracy.

In smaller but no less significant ways, three graduate students at the University of Maryland have helped push this volume to completion. Terrie Hruzd found time amid her studies of Eastern Europe and her duties as administrative assistant of the Freedmen and Southern Society Project to shepherd *Families and Freedom* through corrections, revisions, and modern publishing's maze of technical requirements. Mark Tacyn and Jay Thomas joined her in proofreading text and checking citations. We thank them for their assistance.

Finally, a word should be said for our publisher, André Schiffrin and his staff at The New Press. Our editor, Ellen Reeves, and managing editor, Grace Farrell, did more than their share to guide this volume into print. Eric Banks copyedited and Charles Nix designed a book of which all can be proud. We thank them and salute them for their determination to maintain the highest standards of publishing while creating a new kind of press. We are pleased to be part of that ambitious and laudatory enterprise.

PREFACE

No issue has roiled the study of African-American life more than the character of the family. From the first justifications of African captivity to contemporary debates over welfare policy, scholars and politicos, preachers and plain folk have argued about the strengths and weaknesses of black family life. For some, the trials of the African-American family demonstrate the force of European-American racism; for others, they reveal festering pathologies within black society. For some, they affirm the unyielding undertow of social anarchy; for others, a people's triumph over adversity.

Americans, black and white, have entered this debate at various points. But no matter what the point of entry, the argument has inevitably found its way to the slave family and its transformation during the period of emancipation. *Families and Freedom: A Documentary History of African-American Kinship in the Civil War Era* addresses that long argument.

Families and Freedom draws on the documents assembled by the Freedmen and Southern Society Project from the vast holdings of the National Archives of the United States. For more than twenty years, members of the project—located at the University of Maryland—have been selecting, transcribing, organizing, annotating, and publishing those records in a multivolume series entitled *Freedom: A Documentary History of Emancipation, 1861–1867*. These volumes, which combine documents and interpretive essays, have provided historians with the tools to rethink emancipation and have allowed interested readers to trace the path African Americans followed as they moved from slavery to freedom.

Four hefty volumes of *Freedom* are now in print, as is a companion book of essays, *Slaves No More*. But the very bulk of these works has discouraged some readers. In 1992, to provide easier access to the series, The New Press published an abridgment of the first four volumes of *Freedom*, entitled *Free at Last: A Documentary History of Slavery, Freedom, and the Civil War*. The response has been heartening. The shorter and more accessible format has not only gained a larger readership than the more scholarly *Freedom* volumes, but has also lent itself to classroom use. *Free at Last* has formed the basis of theatrical productions and dramatic readings that have reached radio audiences, school assemblies, members of labor unions, and audiences in libraries, historical societies, museums, businesses, and community groups. It has also encouraged interested parties to consult *Freedom*.

Families and Freedom, like *Free at Last*, draws on documents previously published in the first four volumes of *Freedom*. It also includes documents slated for future volumes that were introduced in a 1988 article in *Radical History Review*. It thus brings together—with new interpretive introductions and headnotes—the most compelling documentation about the African-American family that the Freedmen and Southern Society Project has published to date.

Like its predecessors, *Families and Freedom* is constructed from the extraordinary documentary record created by the crisis that accompanied the American Civil War. That war and the period of reconstruction that followed unleashed the eloquence of the American people and created bureaucracies—the Bureau of Colored Troops, the various federal armies, the Freedmen's Bureau—that collected and preserved the record of that eloquence.

Most of the documents are, of course, mundane iterations of the business of modern warfare and postwar occupation, but buried among the bureaucratic reports that now crowd the shelves of the National Archives are hundreds—perhaps thousands—of letters by slaves and former slaves, many of which speak directly to their concerns as parents and children, husbands and wives, aunts and uncles, and kin of all sorts. This written record—often penned in barely legible scrawls—provides the fullest description of black family life at the moment of emancipation, the deepest understanding of what slaves' domestic life had been in the antebellum South, and the most expansive expression of the aspirations of former slaves and free blacks for themselves and their families. It conveys, as perhaps no historical narrative can, the reshaping of the black family during the transition from slavery to freedom.

EDITORIAL METHOD

The editors have approached the question of transcription with the conviction that readability need not require extensive editorial intervention and, indeed, that modernization (beyond what is already imposed by typesetting) can compromise the historical value of a document.

Therefore, the textual body of each document in this volume is reproduced *exactly* as it appears in the original manuscript—to the extent permitted by modern typography. (Exceptions to this general principle will be noted hereafter.) All peculiarities of syntax, spelling, capitalization, and punctuation appear in the original manuscript. Illegible or obscured words that can be inferred with confidence from textual evidence are printed in ordinary roman type, enclosed in brackets. If the editors' reading is conjectural or doubtful, a question mark is added. When the editors cannot decipher a word by either inference or conjecture, it is represented by a three-dot ellipsis enclosed in brackets. An undecipherable passage of more than one word is represented in the same way, but a footnote reports the extent of the illegible material. (A summary of editorial symbols follows this essay.)

Some adaptations are employed to designate characteristics of handwritten letters that cannot be exactly or economically reproduced on the printed page. Words underlined once in the manuscript appear in *italics*. Words underlined more than once are printed in SMALL CAPITALS. Interlineations are incorporated into the text at the point marked by the author. Finally, the beginning of a new paragraph is indicated by indentation, regardless of how the author set apart paragraphs.

The editors deviate from the standard of faithful reproduction of the textual body of the document in only two significant ways. First, the endings of unpunctuated or unconventionally punctuated sentences are marked with extra space. Second, some documents are not printed in their entirety; each editorial omission is indicated by a four-dot ellipsis.

The editors intervene without notation in the text of manuscripts in three minor ways. When the author of a manuscript inadvertently repeated a word, the duplicate is silently omitted. Similarly, most material crossed out by the author is omitted without note, since it usually represents false starts or ordinary slips of the pen. (When, however, the editors judge that the crossed-out material reflects an important alteration of meaning, it is printed as ~~canceled type~~.) Other editorial interventions in the textual body of a document are clearly identified by being placed in italics and in brackets. These include descriptive interpolations such as [*In another handwriting*] or [*Endorsement*], expansion of unusual abbreviations, the addition of words or letters omitted by the author, and the correction of misspelled words and erroneous dates. The editors exercise restraint in making such additions, however, intervening only when the document cannot be understood or is seriously misleading as it stands. In particular, no effort is made to correct misspelled personal and place names. When material added by the editors is conjectural, a question mark is placed within the brackets.

In the interest of saving space, the editors have adopted the following procedures for treating the peripheral parts of manuscripts. The inside address and return address of a letter are omitted. (Instead, the text preceding each document conveys information about the sender and recipient, and an endnote supplies their names and titles exactly as they appear in the document.) The place and date are printed on a single line at the beginning of the document regardless of where they appear in the manuscript. The salutation and complimentary closing of a letter are run into the text regardless of their positions in the original. Multiple signatures are printed only when there are twelve or fewer names. For documents with more than twelve signatures, the editors indicate only the number of signers, for example, [*86 signatures*]. The formal legal apparatus accompanying documents such as sworn affidavits—including the names of witnesses and the name and position of the official who administered the oath—is omitted without notation. Postscripts that concern matters unrelated to the body of a letter are also silently omitted.

A technical description symbol follows each document, usually on the same line as the signature. This symbol describes the physical form of the manuscript, the handwriting, and the signature. (For a list of the symbols employed, see p. xvii.)

Endnotes provide source citations for the documents published in *Families and Freedom*. When a document has already appeared in *Freedom: A Documentary History of Emancipation*, the endnote indicates the particular volume and pages; there, the reader will find full information regarding its location in the National Archives. Documents that have not yet appeared in *Freedom* are provided with full National Archives citations.

EDITORIAL SYMBOLS

[roman]

Words or letters in roman type within brackets represent editorial inference or conjecture of parts of manuscripts that are illegible, obscured, or mutilated. A question mark indicates doubt about the conjecture.

[. . .]

A three-dot ellipsis within brackets represents illegible or obscured words that the editors cannot decipher. If there is more than one undecipherable word, a footnote reports the extent of the passage.

. . .*

A three-dot ellipsis and a footnote represent words or passages entirely lost because the manuscript is torn or a portion is missing. The footnote reports the approximate amount of material missing.

~~canceled~~

Canceled type represents material written and then crossed out by the author of a manuscript. This device is used only when the editors judge that the crossed-out material reflects an important alteration of meaning. Ordinarily, canceled words are omitted without notation.

[*italic*]

Words or letters in italic type within brackets represent material that has been inserted by the editors and is not part of the original manuscript. A question mark indicates that the insertion is a conjecture.

. . . .

A four-dot ellipsis centered on a separate line represents editorial omission of a substantial body of material. A shorter omission, of only one or two sentences, is indicated by a four-dot ellipsis between two sentences.

SYMBOLS USED
TO DESCRIBE MANUSCRIPTS

Symbols describing the handwriting, form, and signature of each document appear at the end of each document.

The first capital letter describes the handwriting of the document:

A autograph (written in the author's hand)
H handwritten by other than the author (for example, by a clerk)

The second capital letter, with lower-case modifier when appropriate, describes the form of the document:

L letter   c copy
D document   d draft
E endorsement   f fragment

The third capital letter (or its absence) describes the signature:

S signed by the author
Sr signed with a representation of the author's name
I initialed by the author
   no signature or representation

The more common symbols include:

ALS (autograph letter, signed by author), HLS (handwritten letter, signed by author), HLSr (handwritten letter, signed with a representation), HLcSr (handwritten copy of a letter, signed with a representation), HD (handwritten document, no signature).

SHORT TITLES AND ABBREVIATIONS

SHORT TITLES

Black Military Experience
> *Freedom: A Documentary History of Emancipation, 1861–1867.*
> Series 2, *The Black Military Experience*, ed. Ira Berlin, Joseph P.
> Reidy, and Leslie S. Rowland (Cambridge, 1982).

Destruction of Slavery
> *Freedom: A Documentary History of Emancipation, 1861–1867.*
> Series 1, volume 1, *The Destruction of Slavery*, ed. Ira Berlin,
> Barbara J. Fields, Thavolia Glymph, Joseph P. Reidy, and Leslie
> S. Rowland (Cambridge, 1985).

Official Records
> U.S., War Department, *The War of the Rebellion: A Compilation of
> the Official Records of the Union and Confederate Armies*, 128 vols.
> (Washington, 1880–1901).

Statutes at Large
> United States, *Statutes at Large, Treaties, and Proclamations of the United States of America*, 17 vols. (Boston, 1850–73).

Wartime Genesis: Lower South
> *Freedom: A Documentary History of Emancipation, 1861–1867.* Series 1, volume 3, *The Wartime Genesis of Free Labor: The Lower South*, ed. Ira Berlin, Thavolia Glymph, Steven F. Miller, Joseph P. Reidy, Leslie S. Rowland, and Julie Saville (Cambridge, 1990).

Wartime Genesis: Upper South
> *Freedom: A Documentary History of Emancipation, 1861–1867.* Series 1, volume 2, *The Wartime Genesis of Free Labor: The Upper South*, ed. Ira Berlin, Steven F. Miller, Joseph P. Reidy, and Leslie S. Rowland (Cambridge, 1993).

ABBREVIATIONS

Asst.	*Assistant*	Hd. Qrs.	*Headquarters*
Brig.	*Brigadier*	Hon.	*Honorable*
BRFAL	*Bureau of Refugees, Freedmen, and Abandoned Lands (Freedmen's Bureau)*	Inf., Inft., Infy.	*Infantry*
		inst.	*instant; i.e., of the current month*
Capt.	*Captain*	Lt., Lieut.	*Lieutenant*
C.H.	*Court House*	Maj.	*Major*
Co.	*Company*	obt. servt.	*obedient servant*
Co.	*County*	Regt.	*Regiment*
Col.	*Colonel*	Sergt., Sgt.	*Sergeant*
col^d, cold.	*colored*	Supt.	*Superintendent*
comdg.	*commanding*	USCI	*U.S. Colored Infantry*
Dept.	*Department*	USCT	*U.S. Colored Troops*
Dist.	*District*	Vols.	*Volunteers (usually preceded by a state abbreviation)*
Engrs.	*Engineers*		
Gen., Gen'l	*General*	&c	*et cetera*

FAMILIES AND FREEDOM

INTRODUCTION

From the beginning of African slavery in mainland North America, black people understood their society in the idiom of kinship. During the long years of bondage, African-American families transmitted African culture from the Old World to the New, socialized the young and succored the old, buffered relations with masters and mistresses, and served as engines of resistance to an oppressive regime. Early on, African-American slaves extended the bonds of kinship beyond the boundaries of individual households, uniting family members who were forced to live apart by the circumstances of their enslavement. The language of kinship expressed a broad range of mutual obligations. Slaves addressed each other as brothers and sisters, uncles and aunts, conferring the status of kin on men and women who were unrelated by blood or marriage. By the middle of the eighteenth century, kinship ideology and practices had extended to the larger African-American community. For most slaves, familial and communal relations were one.

Yet in many respects, the African-American family was the most fragile of institutions. The slave regime of the American South gave slaves little room to develop a family life. Slaves' marriages had no legal standing; their unions were mere couplings whose issue, like the slaves' labor, belonged to their owners. In the eyes of the law, slaves could not be husbands and wives, fathers and mothers. Slave parents had no rights to their children, who—like themselves—were the owner's property. Since the owner's rights were preeminent, slave parents lacked authority to discipline their children or sustain their aged parents. Among slaves, kinship ties were simple fictions that no one need respect, certainly not the slaveowner.

Backed by the power of the state and a monopoly of legal force, slaveowners projected themselves as the fictive fathers and mothers of the slave community. It was the owners—who preferred the titles "master" and "mistress" precisely because of their domestic connotations—rather than their fathers and mothers of birth, to whom slave children were taught to defer and whom they were expected to love. It was the owners who fed, clothed, and sheltered slave children and who established the regulations and articulated the values that would govern their lives. As if to confirm this harsh reality, slaveowners often contradicted and superseded slave parents in matters of disciplining and directing slave children. Indeed, slave children regularly saw slaveholders chastise their parents, a chilling lesson about the source of domestic—as well as plantation—governance and authority.

Often the slaveholders' commitment to their own preeminence took the insidious form of manipulating the slaves' desire for a modicum of domestic security. From the owners' perspective, regular family relations made slaves less rebellious, inasmuch as domestic ties gave them something to protect. No threat was more effective in bringing an unruly slave to heel than the intimation that failure to yield to the owner's wishes would mean sale, separation, and the permanent loss of loved ones. Furthermore, domestic stability appeared to promote the growth of the slave population, adding to the slaveholders' wealth. By allowing slaves to establish family ties, slaveholders strengthened the plantation regime.

Much as slaveowners likened themselves to concerned, even loving parents and found their own interests served by domestic regularity in the slave quarter, they understood that the business of domination was a brutal one. The lash, the paddle, the branding iron, and the stocks were necessities, since slaves continually resisted their rule. Slaveholders also acknowledged that at times they—or at least some of their number—overstepped the bounds needed to gain obedience. Some did so out of anger, some out of lust, and some from the perverse pleasure of brutalizing men and women they considered barely human. While many owners deplored such barbarism and worked to eliminate it, even the fiercest defenders of the slave regime recognized the unfortunate reality.

The slaveholders' interest in encouraging family connections in the quarter was also compromised by decisions to sell or transfer slaves. Such decisions might be the calculated result of a reorganization of plantation production or a hasty response to financial crisis; they might derive from an owner's death or from a determination to punish an intractable slave. Whatever the cause, such transfers—mere property transactions in the plantation account book—inevitably fragmented families.

Few slaves escaped the pain of forcible separation from their kin, especially during the nineteenth century. The spread of cotton cultivation across the Lower South resulted in the removal or sale of some one million slaves from their homes in the seaboard states, deeply disrupting the civilization that black people had established in the aftermath of their forced exodus from Africa. The westward migration tore black families asunder, as households and sometimes whole communities dissolved under the pressure of the cotton revolution. In the older states of the Upper South, few slaves could expect to see their children grow to maturity; in the newer states of the Lower South, many slaves had neither siblings, parents, nor grandparents in residence.

Within the plantation, slaveholders had innumerable means at their disposal to disrupt slaves' domestic life. Rations could be allotted and clothing dispersed in ways that created envy and competition among kin, work could be assigned that left parents no time to tend to infant children, older children could be removed from their parents to labor in the Big House, and parents could be ridiculed and shamed before their children. But perhaps the most detested manifestation of the slaveholders' power was the usurpation of the marriage bed and the sexual violation of young people, particularly young women.

Slavery thus played havoc with the domestic lives of slaves. The inability of parents to protect their children and to provide for loved ones eroded their domestic authority and their capacity to impart their own values to their offspring. In like manner, the slaves' inability to hold—rather than be—property and the resulting absence of a system of legal inheritance denied the slave family a material base and eroded long-term loyalties. The owners' power stunted generational ties within the slave community, as slaves were dealt from master to master and from plantation to plantation like so many cards in a game of chance.

Slaves resisted the reduction of their domestic life to a mere extension of the owner's will, refusing, as best they could, to allow their most intimate and treasured relationships to be hostage to their owner's whim. Like the slaveholders, slaves recognized that the struggle for "mastery" literally began at home and understood that only their ability to govern families of their own would free them from their owner's claim. Thus, in the teeth of the slaveholder's power—and the state's authority, which buttressed that power—slaves entered into conjugal unions, established families, and articulated values that contradicted those of the owners or selectively appropriated the owners' values to their own advantage. Ultimately the slave family became the primary bulwark against the master's rule. It sowed the seeds of the destruction of chattel bondage.

Slaves based their family life on the marriage compact. They courted according to customs of their own choosing and selected partners according to rules of their own making—rarely, for example, marrying first cousins or other close kin, a practice that was common among the slave-holding class. Once married, most slave husbands and wives honored their vows with lifelong fidelity. Their unions were broken more often by death or forcible separation than by desertion or mutual agreement. Within the slave household, husbands and wives played distinct and complementary roles, which—although frequently strained by the realities of chattel bondage and sometimes disrupted by violence—enriched the material and emotional lives of both partners. To supplement the owner's dole, husbands hunted and fished and crafted furniture, shoes, and tools, and wives fashioned their own wares as quilters, weavers, and seam-stresses. Together they worked gardens and provision grounds, kept barnyard animals, made pottery, and wove baskets. Sometimes they sold their produce and handicrafts to fellow slaves, to their owners, or to other free people. Slave men and women thus divided some tasks within the household and shared others, creating their own sexual division of labor.

The division of labor within the household was never fixed, however, for the slave family was not a static institution. The roles of men and women within the family changed over time, and differed from place to place, depending on the demands of particular crops, the size of the unit on which slaves resided, the possibility of joint residence, and, of course, the intrusive power of the master and mistress.

Most slave children were born into two-parent households, generally with the help of a slave midwife. The slave community condemned some relationships as illegitimate, although it rarely shamed women who bore children out of wedlock and almost never failed to accept those children. Nonetheless, censure of some relationships affirmed the legitimacy of others and attested to the central function of the slave family. Slave parents—often in direct conflict with their owners—took responsibility for their children from birth. They named them, nurtured them through infancy, guided them though childhood, and led them through the various—and dangerous—rites of passage whereby children became "hands" and took their place in the owners' kitchens, workshops, and fields. By tutoring their children in the complex etiquette necessary to survive in the violent and exploitative world of slavery, slave parents clarified the differences between masters and parents. In passing to manhood or womanhood, slave children became members of both the plantation community and the slave community, but—from their parents' perspective—there could be no doubts as to where loyalty should rest. In this they were remarkably successful: Many slaves named their children after their parents, grandparents, aunts, and uncles; few named them after their owners.

Husbands and wives divided the labor of childrearing among themselves. Much turned on the question of residence, for while many slave husbands and wives shared the same cabin, others—in some places, a majority—belonged to different owners and resided miles apart. But whether parents lived together or not, most of the responsibilities of childrearing fell to mothers. Fathers also played an important role in the lives of slave children, and, perhaps to strengthen the more distant tie, children were more often named for their fathers than their mothers.

Still, sale, death, and divided residence limited the ability of husbands and wives to shepherd their progeny to adulthood. To ensure that their children would be raised in accordance with their wishes, slave parents called on other members of their community. Slaves understood that at any time they might be required to assume the role of mother or father, aunt or uncle, for a child to whom they were unconnected by blood or marriage. Children sold from one plantation were generally adopted into the households on another. Such fosterage, moreover, was not limited to long-term separations, but might be initiated as a result of short-term illness or the seasonal absence of a parent. In recognition of the large roles played by fictive kin, slaves invested such men and women with the titles of "aunt" and "uncle," esteemed appellations within the slave quarter. Large-scale fosterage and fictive kinship knit community and household together, making them one.

Slaves nurtured these connections in various ways. Although they could legally hold no property, they nonetheless developed systems of gifting and inheritance, which, like the customs that regulated courtship and mate selection, existed outside the owner's purview and the state's laws. The generational transfer of property was small by any measure—a quilt, a few sticks of furniture, a treasured tool or cooking pot, but often included barnyard animals like chickens and hogs. These tokens not only held enormous emotional value but also gave young people "a start," enabling them to reproduce the household economies that enriched their parents' life.

Slaves recognized that their owners had an interest in maintaining a modicum of family stability on the plantation. They manipulated to their own benefit the slaveowners' belief that regular family relations made for good business. Slaves thus turned the owners' self-interest against them in petitioning to reside with a spouse, to visit an ailing relative, or to cele-brate a wedding in the quarter. When they could, they reinforced the slaveowners' understanding that productivity and social peace required that slave family life be undisturbed by meddling from above. They made the point by objecting violently to such interference. Slaveholders came to appreciate that the greatest source of flight and other disorder was the division of families.

Slaves valued their family ties. Marriage was a joyous occasion, as was the birth of a child—which represented renewed hope that the next gen-eration would live to celebrate the "Day of Jubilee" when all would be free at last. Severance of the bonds of kinship was a grievous loss. Slaves reserved their harshest judgment against their owners not for insuffi-cient food, shabby clothing, inadequate shelter, overwork, or even gratu-itous violence but for playing havoc with their families. Slaves never for-got the husbands and wives, mothers and fathers, brothers and sisters, and other kin who were sold away. Many slaves carried in their minds detailed genealogies that reached back generations, sometimes to an African root. That familial root, which nurtured people of African descent through the years of bondage, also shaped their vision of a future in freedom.

The slave family reflected the basic contradiction of an institution that defined men and women as property, a contradiction that has divided his-torians considering slave family life. Reflecting on the legal constraints and the asymmetry of power between master and slave, many have con-cluded that the slave family was of little consequence. To argue other-wise, they maintain, denies the brutal reality of slavery. Although these scholars concede that some men and women may have tried to create a meaningful domestic life under barbarous conditions, their efforts were doomed to failure. Such heroic struggles might be admired, but to presume that they succeeded was romantic fantasy purveyed by either softheaded sentimentalists or unabashed apologists for southern slavery. Wrapping themselves in the mantle of realism, these historians see the glass as half empty. They emphasize the violent, destructive character of chattel bondage and the damage it inflicted on black people.

For other scholars, the glass was half full. Recognizing the horrific circumstances of slaves' domestic life, these historians are impressed by the dense web of family ties slaves spun and the system of values they created in contradistinction to that of their owners. Reflecting on what slaves created in practice, such historians deny the charges of romanticism or apology. Instead, they claim for themselves the banner of realism, maintaining that actions rather than laws are a better test of historical reality. While not denying the brutality of slavery, these historians measure the slaves' achievement not only by what they did but also by what they did with what they had. To them, the slave family was neither romantic vision nor sentimentalist sop, but the central reality of African-American life.

Was the glass half empty or half full or perhaps both? This volume addresses that question while providing direct evidence of the structure of African-American family life during the transition from slavery to freedom and the beliefs of black people respecting marriage, children, and the obligations of kinship. Two introductory documents put the matter in sharp focus.

———•———

Jean Baptiste Roudanez was among the quarter of a million southerners of African descent who were already free at the time of the Civil War. As publisher of the New Orleans *Tribune* and a prominent member of the city's community of educated, bilingual *gens de*

couleur, Roudanez took a keen interest in the changes that accompanied emancipation. In 1864, he shared his views about family life
under slavery with a War Department commission investigating
the condition of former slaves in the parts of the Confederacy that
had been occupied by Union forces.

New Orleans [*La.*]   Feb 9th 1864

Deposition of J. B. Roudanez, a Creole mulatto, of New Orleans.

For many years I was employed as a mechanic on plantations;   I am
thoroughly acquainted with slave life on the plantations;   in general, the
slaves have one given name, to which they affix that of their
master;   the colored families are not always kept together; some have
their families with them, but the family relation is not well maintained;
the slaves are not permitted to eat at a family table; under the old
French rule, rations were served out to persons; as a general custom, of
late years, the cooking was done for the entire force by regular details;
the negroes came with their buckets, got their share, and ate it by
themselves;   they were lodged in cabins built for them;   they fixed beds
for themselves, and made their own furniture;   there were generally two
or four rooms to cabins; one room would be given to a family;   the young
people were lodged separately, but married couples lodged by
themselves;   families had usually a room twelve feet square;   in relation
to child-bearing, the feeling of planters was divergent; some planters
desired the negro women to have children, and some did not;   some
planters worked the women as hard as the men; in some instances they
were obliged to labor in every stage of conception;   these statements
relate exclusively to the sugar plantations;   the planters were indifferent
in regard to the chastity of their negresses; there were many illicit
children;   generally speaking, the young masters were criminally

intimate with the negro girls; it was their custom;   the girls copulate at
fourteen years, and under; have known girls to be mothers at that
age;   some of the French planters had children by slave women;   the
planters' sons preferred these half-sisters for concubines;   the practice
of copulation was so frequent among negro girls that a chaste one at
seventeen years was almost unknown;   some were kept at work while
with child, and others sent to labor one week after confinement;
sometimes they were compelled to labor up to the moment of conception;
they usually performed men's labor; to this there were some exceptions;
ordinarily, they were given one month to recover;   mothers were
permitted to nurse children one half hour three times a day;   have
heard, but do not know, of women being taken with labor pains in the
field;   slavery on the plantations had no regard for family relations.

As to punishments and discipline: Some planters were very severe; in
these matters there was a great difference;   whipping was the common
mode;   some were confined at night in the stocks for days or weeks; they
were whipped with a paddle usually;   a paddle is a piece of wood about
sixteen inches in length, covered with sole leather nailed over it to the
width of a hand; this was used when it was not wished to mark the slave;
when the paddle was used the negro was stripped naked and held by
others;   both sexes were subject to this species of punishment;   the
number of blows was prescribed in advance, and were inflicted on the
posterior; 16 to 30 was the usual number;   sometimes a whip was used;
this is made of cowhide; is seven feet long, and has a hempen cord with
knots for a lash; the cord is about 1/8 of an inch in thickness; the lash
was a foot in length;   when whipped, they were stripped from the middle
of the back downward;   still another mode of punishment was to put
round the neck an iron collar with branches one foot in length;   heavy
iron rings were also put round the legs, with a chain tied up to the knee;

these were common methods of punishment; I have heard of negroes having been bound to stakes and given two or three hundred lashes; have heard of instances of great cruelty to negroes; sometimes women with child were forced to lie down and receive the lash—a hole being dug underneath them large enough to admit the pregnant stomach; negroes were sometimes branded with the owner's mark; on some plantations this was done with a red hot iron; ears were sometimes clipped to show ownership; between the wife and favorite women of the planter there was often the greatest jealousy; the planters were generally in the habit of cohabiting with their slave women; in consequence wives often made false statements against these favorites and had them whipped; for fear they would not be punished, wives often had them whipped in their presence; the slave relation was often the source of great domestic difficulty; the fact of cohabitation was well known to both parents and children; there was no provision for the instruction of the negroes; none was permitted; the planter did not desire to have their negroes become religious; many secret religious meetings were held; they were dispersed when the facts were ascertained; they would frequently repair to the woods to pray; as a general rule, they are very religious; their general character for truth is good; they are not in the habit of lying; they sometimes had not enough to eat or to wear, and in consequence would take what was needed; in general they were not thieves; one-fourth to one-tenth of the negroes are colored; I know some plantations where one-half or three-fourths are colored; many colored children were the offspring of planters; these were generally made house servants; I think the pure negro lives the longest; I have known both negro and colored women to have fifteen children each; slave women prefer to cohabit with white men rather than black; mixed children are considered more creditable; the

negroes are much more virtuous since the Proclamation of
Freedom;   the females are more chaste, because an honest livelihood is
open to them;   cohabitation was prompted by the wants of the colored
women; such as dress, clothing, etc.;   their religious instruction is much
better than formerly;   they are fond of religious meetings, and generally
attend them;   there are very few freemen who have not joined
themselves to some religious society;   they are mostly Methodists and
Baptists;   among those born in the State Catholicism universally
prevails;   an idea obtained from the old Spanish settlers yet retains its
hold: horse-shoes are nailed upon the door-steps to insure good luck.

The hours of labor on sugar plantations are from fifteen to eighteen
hours per day for the year;   at certain seasons they are obliged to labor a
great part of the night;   they are usually called at 3 or 4 A.M.;   overseers
have power over all field hands;   those inside the house yard are house
servants;   the overseer is usually expected to produce a certain crop
with a fixed number of hands;   all are obliged to obey him in preference
to the master;   he is generally much more cruel than the master;   kind-
hearted planters sometimes select cruel overseers;   sometimes a field
hand is called away by the master, when he is whipped by the overseer
for obeying the planter; should he refuse his master, *he* would whip him;
as a general rule, overseers have intercourse with the slave women; if
one resists, some occasion is found for her punishment;   bloodhounds
are in ordinary use for catching runaway slaves; *some whites make this
a profession.*

As to the present management and conduct of the officers having the
freemen in charge here and on the plantations—more especially Provost
Marshals,—I am free to declare that they have not done justice to the
slaves; they do not see that Gen. Banks's orders are carried out;   on
many places whipping is still permitted;   in October last a slave was

beaten by his master with a stick; he complained to Capt. O'Brien, Provost Marshal of the parish of St. James, who took him home and helped his master to wash his head; he then told the negro to stay there and the master would not again whip him;　many employers last year cheated the negroes out of their wages;　I think it best for the negro that his remuneration be left open to competition; also better for the employer.　In some instances last year the planters paid their negroes more than was prescribed; both parties were perfectly satisfied; the order requiring the laborers to remain for one year upon the plantations where they engage is, in my opinion, right.

Generally speaking, the condition of the colored people has greatly improved since their freedom was acknowledged;　they endeavor to find employment;　they appreciate their newly-discovered rights very highly; I think if left free in a community by themselves they would be capable of self-government;　they will endeavor to their utmost ability to discharge satisfactorily their civil duties;　they have no idea of government;　often they discuss political questions;　in Louisiana they have had a certain kind of political education;　they often discuss the question of the fitness of their respective masters to hold political power; there are one or more on each plantation who have secretly learned to read;　they secretly read newspapers;　the day following that on which the news of the execution of John Brown reached New Orleans I sat out for a plantation 75 miles distant; a slave gave me the details of the execution;　a negro in the sugar-house asked the master for a paper to clean some machinery, and he retained and read it; he secretly read it to the entire force;　whenever a slave was known to be able to read and write he was punished severely.[1]

HD

Although Hawkins Wilson, an ex-slave in Texas, had been sold away from Virginia as a teenager, time and distance had neither dimmed his memories of childhood family and friends nor diminished his emotional connection to them. Twenty-four years after their forced separation, he wrote to his "dearest relatives" through the Freedmen's Bureau, introducing himself to them not as the boy they had known but as the man he had become. His letters reveal both the terrible burden slavery placed on the stability of black families and the centrality of kinship in the lives of the slaves.

[*Galveston, Tex.*]   May 11th, 1867—

Dear Sir,   I am anxious to learn about my sisters, from whom I have been separated many years—   I have never heard from them since I left Virginia twenty four years ago—   I am in hopes that they are still living and I am anxious to hear how they are getting on—   I have no other one to apply to but you and am persuaded that you will help one who stands in need of your services as I do—   I shall be very grateful to you, if you oblige me in this matter—   One of my sisters belonged to Peter Coleman in Caroline County and her name was Jane—   Her husband's name was Charles and he belonged to Buck Haskin and lived near John Wright's store in the same county—   She had three children, Robert, Charles and Julia, when I left—   Sister Martha belonged to Dr Jefferson, who lived two miles above Wright's store—   Sister Matilda belonged to Mrs. Botts, in the same county—   My dear uncle Jim had a wife at Jack Langley's and his wife was named Adie and his oldest son was named Buck and they all belonged to Jack Langley—   These are all my own dearest relatives and I wish to correspond with them with a view to visit them as soon as I can hear from them—   My name is Hawkins Wilson and I am their brother, who was sold at Sheriff's sale and used to belong to Jackson Talley and was bought by M. Wright,

Boydtown C.H.   You will please send the enclosed letter to my sister
Jane, or some of her family, if she is dead— I am, very respectfully,
your obedient servant,

ALS   Hawkins Wilson—

[*Enclosure*]   [*Galveston, Tex.   May 11, 1867*]
Dear Sister Jane,   Your little brother Hawkins is trying to find out
where you are and where his poor old mother is— Let me know and I
will come to see you— I shall never forget the bag of buiscuits you
made for me the last night I spent with you— Your advice to me to
meet you in Heaven has never passed from my mind and I have
endeavored to live as near to my God, that if He saw fit not to suffer us
to meet on earth, we might indeed meet in Heaven— I was married in
this city on the 10th March 1867 by Rev. Samuel Osborn to Mrs.
Martha White, a very intelligent and lady-like woman— You may
readily suppose that I was not fool enough to marry a Texas girl— My
wife was from Georgia and was raised in that state and will make me
very happy— I have learned to read, and write a little— I teach
Sunday School and have a very interesting class— If you do not mind,
when I come, I will astonish you in religious affairs— I am sexton of
the Methodist Episcopal Church colored— I hope you and all my
brothers and sisters in Virginia will stand up to this church; for I expect
to live and die in the same— When I meet you, I shall be as much
overjoyed as Joseph was when he and his father met after they had been
separated so long— Please write me all the news about you all— I am
writing tonight all about myself and I want you to do likewise about your
and my relations in the state of Virginia— Please send me some of
Julia's hair whom I left a baby in the cradle when I was torn away from
you— I know that she is a young lady now, but I hope she will not deny

her affectionate uncle this request, seeing she was an infant in the cradle when he saw her last— Tell Mr. Jackson Talley how-do-ye and give my love to all his family, Lucy, Ellen and Sarah— Also to my old playmate Henry Fitz who used to play with me and also to all the colored boys who, I know, have forgotten me, but I have not forgotten them— I am writing to you tonight, my dear sister, with my Bible in my hand praying Almighty God to bless you and preserve you and me to meet again— Thank God that now we are not sold and torn away from each other as we used to be— we can meet if we see fit and part if we like— Think of this and praise God and the Lamb forever— I will now present you a little prayer which you will say every night before you go to sleep— Our father who art in heaven &c, you will know what the rest is— Dear sister, I have had a rugged road to travel, since I parted with you, but thank God, I am happy now, for King Jesus is my Captain and God is my friend. He goes before me as a pillar of fire by night and a cloud by day to lead me to the New Jerusalem where all is joy, and happiness and peace— Remember that we have got to meet before that great triune God— My reputation is good before white and black. I am chief of all the turnouts of the colored people of Galveston— Last July 1866, I had the chief command of four thousand colored people of Galveston— So you may know that I am much better off, than I used to be when I was a little shaver in Caroline, running about in my shirt tail picking up chips— Now, if you were to see me in my fine suit of broadcloth, white kid gloves and long red sash, you would suppose it was Gen. Schofield marching in parade uniform into Richmond— The 1st day of May, 1867, I had 500 colored people, big and little, again under my command— We had a complete success and were complimented by Gen. Griffin and Mr. Wheelock the superintendent of the colored schools of Texas— We expect to have a picnic for the Sunday School soon— I

am now a grown man weighing one hundred and sixty odd pounds— I
am wide awake and full of fun, but I never forget my duty to my God—
I get eighteen dollars a month for my services as sexton and eighteen
dollars a week outside— I am working in a furniture shop and will fix
up all your old furniture for you, when I come to Virginia if you have
any— I work hard all the week— On Sunday I am the first one in the
church and the last to leave at night; being all day long engaged in
serving the Lord; teaching Sunday School and helping to worship God—
Kind sister, as paper is getting short and the night is growing old and I
feel very weak in the eyes and I have a great deal to do before I turn in
to bed and tomorrow I shall have to rise early to attend Sunday School, I
must come to a conclusion— Best love to yourself and inquiring
friends— Write as quickly as you can and direct to Hawkins Wilson
care of Methodist Episcopal church, colored, Galveston, Texas— Give
me your P. Office and I will write again— I shall drop in upon you
some day like a thief in the night.— I bid you a pleasant night's rest
with a good appetite for your breakfast and no breakfast to eat— Your
loving and affectionate brother—

ALS   Hawkins Wilson[2]

> Hawkins Wilson's letters were forwarded to the Freedmen's
> Bureau agent in Carolina County, Virginia—in whose files they
> remain, suggesting that his kinfolk were never found.

CHAPTER

I.

ESCAPE, RESCUE, AND RECAPTURE:

FAMILIES AND THE WARTIME STRUGGLE FOR FREEDOM

AFTER MORE THAN TWO CENTURIES OF AMERI-can captivity, the Civil War allowed black people to claim their freedom. Even before the first shots at Fort Sumter, South Carolina, in April 1861, slaves presented themselves at federal posts, declared their willingness to aid the Union cause, and demanded protection and freedom in return. At first, they were brusquely turned away, as federal authorities from President Abraham Lincoln on down insisted that the conflict was a war for national unity and nothing more. Slaves persisted, understanding full well that their future—and that of their posterity—rested on their ability to seize the moment. In time, they found acceptance in federal camps, for common soldiers valued their services even if high-ranking officers did not. The designation "contraband," which became attached to fugitive slaves, implied that they were no longer slaves but nonetheless still property; it thus represented the federal government's willingness to seize runaways for its own purposes but its reluctance to emancipate them. Slowly, however, the importance of black people to the Union cause—their willingness to labor, their ability to provide information, their readiness to fight—became evident to all but the most obtuse commanders, and fugitive slaves found an increasingly friendly reception within Union lines. The name "contraband" stuck, even as the slaves' chances of gaining legal title to freedom increased under the terms of congressional legislation and presidential proclamation. Finally, in December 1865, the Thirteenth Amendment to the U.S. Constitution abolished chattel slavery forever.

The decision to flee slavery was a family concern, since it frequently meant separation from loved ones unable to hazard the dangers. Those who fled—at first young men with few family obligations—and those who remained behind, generally old people and women encumbered with young children, knew that the pain of parting would be accompanied by the risks of escape. Fugitive slaves might be captured, punished, resold, or executed, and those at home would surely become objects of the slaveholders' ire. Even when owners did not retaliate directly, the remaining slaves faced additional work, as the duties of those who left became the responsibilities of those who stayed. By the second year of the war, such retaliation, on the one hand, and the increasingly friendly reception runaways received within federal lines, on the other, inspired many slaves to flee in family groups. In the war's first year, however, escape divided more families than it united.

———◆———

For John Boston, a runaway slave from Maryland who found refuge with a New York regiment, the exhilaration that accompanied his own liberation was tainted by the resulting separation from his wife and family.

Upton Hill [*Va.*]   January ^{the} 12 1862

My Dear Wife   it is with grate joy I take this time to let you know
Whare I am   i am now in Safety in the 14th Regiment of
Brooklyn   this Day i can Adress you thank god as a free man   I had
a little truble in giting away But as the lord led the Children of Isrel to
the land of Canon So he led me to a land Whare fredom Will rain in spite
Of earth and hell   Dear you must make your Self content i am free

from al the Slavers Lash   and as you have chose the Wise plan Of
Serving the lord i hope you Will pray Much and i Will try by the help of
god To Serv him With all my hart   I am With a very nice man and have
All that hart Can Wish But My Dear I Cant express my grate desire
that i Have to See you   i trust the time Will Come When We Shal meet
again   And if We dont met on earth We Will Meet in heven Whare
Jesas ranes   Dear Elizabeth tell Mrs Own[ees] That i trust that She
Will Continue Her kindness to you and that god Will Bless her on earth
and Save her In grate eternity   My Acomplements To Mrs Owens and
her Children   may They Prosper through life   I never Shall forgit
her kindness to me   Dear Wife i must Close   rest yourself Contented
i am free   i Want you to rite To me Soon as you Can Without
Delay   Direct your letter to the 14th Reigment New york State malitia
Uptons Hill Virginea In Care of M[r] Cranford Comary   Write my Dear
Soon As you C   Your Affectionate Husban   Kiss Daniel For me

John Boston

Give my love to Father and Mother[1]

ALS

> It is not known whether Elizabeth Boston was a free woman or a
> slave, nor is it clear whether she ever read her husband's letter.
> Intercepted before or after she received it, the letter came into the
> hands of a committee of the Maryland House of Delegates, which
> presented it to the Union general-in-chief, George B. McClellan,
> and demanded to know how John Boston's owner, "a loyal citizen
> of Maryland," could recover his fugitive slave.[2]

———•———

> Even when within Union lines, fugitive slaves could never feel
> secure. Grandison Briscoe escaped to the District of Columbia with
> his mother, pregnant wife, and child, but within days a slave

Upton Hill January the 12 1862

My Dear Wife it is with grate joy I take this time to let you know Whare I am i am now in Safety in the 14th Regiment of Brooklyn this Day i can Adress you thank god as a free man I had a little trable in gitingaway But as the lord led the Children of Izrel to the land of Canon So he led me To a land Whare fredom Will rain in spite Of earth and hell Dear you must make your Self content i am free from al the Slavers Lash and as you have chose the Wise plan Of Serving the lord i hope you Will pray Much and i Will try by the help of god To Serv X him With all my hart I am With a very nice man and have All that hart Can Wish But My Dear I Cant express my grate desire that i Have to See you i trust the time Will Come When We Shal meet again And if We dont met on earth We Will Meet in heven Whare Jesas raines

Letter from John Boston

Dear Elizabeth Tell Mrs Owens
That i trust that She Will Continue
Her kindness to you and that god
Will Bless her on earth and Save her
In grate eternity My Complements
To Mrs Owens and her Children may
They Prosper through life I never
Shall forgit her kindness to me

Dear Wife i must Close rest your self
Contented i am free i Want you to rite
To me Soon as you Can With out Delay
Direct your letter to the 14th Reigment
Write my Dear Soon New york State malitia
As you b Uptons Hill
Your Affectionate Husban Virginia
Kiss Daniel For me
John Boston In Care of Mr Cranford
Give my love to Father and Comary
Mother

to Elizabeth Boston. (See pp. 22–23)

catcher dragged his loved ones back into bondage. Nearly two years after their recapture, Briscoe made the following affidavit describing the fate of his family.

[*Washington, D.C.*]   6th day of February 1864

Grandison Briskoe being duly sworn says he is about 25 years of age was born in Maryland & has been married to his wife since 1861   Came to reside with his wife in this City in April—4th day of April 1862 & has resided in said City Since that period of time except a part of the time   he has been in the Service of the United States all the time & is now in Said Service in Virginia—   That his wife & his mother were taken away from Washington in April (on the 7th day) 1862 & as fugitive Slaves & taken to Piscatawa to Broad Creek to their master's [farm?] whose name is John Hunter & My mothers masters name was & is Robert Hunter—   They were both taken to the barn & severely whipped   Their clothes were raised & tied over their heads to keep their screams from disturbing the neighborhood & then were tied up & whipped very severely whipped and then taken to Upper Marlborough to jail   My wife had a Child about nine month's old which was taken from her & died soon after.   Some six or eight months after my wife was imprisoned she had a Child but the inhuman master & mistress though the knew she was soon to be Confined or give birth to a Child made no arrangements provided no Clothing nor anything for the Child or mother   I have sent them Clothing & other articles frequently until the first or near the first of January 1864 Since which the new jailor has refused to allow them to receive any thing from me

They have been in prison for the Crime of Coming to Washington to reside, ever since about the fourth of April 1862 now a year & ten months.   They are confined in Jail at Upper Marlborough Prince George's County Maryland

HDS   Grandison Briscoe[3]

The escape of young, vigorous slaves angered slaveholders, who turned on their families. Nathan McKinney, a successful escapee in Union-occupied New Orleans, discovered that his wife had been jailed and his infant child reclaimed by his owner. Desperate to free his wife from prison and reunite his family, McKinney asked the federal commander in Louisiana for assistance.

Neworleans [*La.*]   Feb th 2 1863

kin Sire   I wash to state to you this morning the hole mattor   I am in truble and like Jacob of old and Can not let the go untill you Comford me   My wife and felloservent was orded to go to yeenkis and they left and went and sence that they hav taken them and put them in prison taken the mother from hire Suckling Child put the mother in and taken the Child home   I and my wife and felloservent am not willing to go Back   we had Rented a house and living in it 20 Days then taken   if you please Sire gave me a premiat to gat my wife out of Prison and my things out off his house the no 262 Cannal St mrs George Ruleff Reseadents   your most obodent Servent

ALS   Nathan mc kinney[4]

Fugitive slaves who reached Union lines did not forget those left behind. A Missouri slaveholder denounced the actions of escaped slaves who, operating from a Union post, obtained arms and sallied forth to liberate their families. The aggrieved master requested relief from General Samuel R. Curtis, the region's federal comman-der, whose response suggested only tepid concern for developments that slaveholders considered dangerous in the extreme.

Jackson Missouri   February 24 1863

Sir   The Federal military by an Act of Congress are prohibited from returning to their owners, slaves escapeing from them and seeking

Fugitive slaves coming into Union lines. (*Harper's Weekly*, Jan. 31, 1863)

refuge in the Federal lines.* Hundreds from this and the adjoining
Counties have escaped and sought protection, within the Federal lines at
the Post at Cape Girardeau— A great many of those thus escapeing
are yet there. Whenever they wish to release a relative from bondage,
they issue out from that place, as I understand, armed, and by menace
take property of that description from the owners— Many instances of
that kind have occurred. About two weeks since, five were taken from
an aged citizen of this County, resideing about five miles from this
place— On last night, I have heard, six negroes, four armed, about 12
oclock rescued some three or four, from the residence of a citizen about
two & a half miles from here— On the same night about nine oclock my
residence was visited by two negroes, entrance demanded and the
delivery up of a small girl (the only one I have)   on my refusal, the
threat was made, that the soldiers would come & take her— On my
replying I would go and see the Colonel (Lieut. Col. Sayear commanding
a detached portion of the Mo S[tate]. M[ilitia]. stationed at this place)
they left. So long as that Regiment remains here, I do not believe such
conduct will be tolerated. If they are removed, the citizens of town have
no more surety for their lives and property, than those of the country—
Surely, the Act of Congress never contemplated or intended to sanction
the abstracting of property in this way.

Under this belief, I would respectfully call the attention of the
Commander in Chief of this Division, to the facts, that a number of
escaped negroes are at the Post at Cape Girardeau—that they come out
of the lines of that Post armed,—that the inhabitants of the County,
generally are unarmed. and that those escaped negroes, can not only
take by force or menace, negroes from their owners; but, if so disposed,

---

*An article of war adopted by Congress in March 1862 forbade members
of the army and navy to return fugitive slaves to their owners. The
Second Confiscation Act of July 17, 1862, reiterated and expanded on
that prohibition. (*Statutes at Large*, vol. 12, pp. 354, 589–92.)

may rob and plunder *ad libitem*.   I do not know that the Commander of the Post at Capt Girardeau has knowledge of these things; and under the circumstances, I would respectfully submit, if you as Commander in Chief, could not put a stop to this state of affairs, by issueing an order, prohibitting negroes carrying arms or leaving the lines of the Post either armed or unarmed unless on lawful business and by a special permit from the Provost Martial, or could not those escaped negroes be removed to some point, where their services are needed by the Goverment.   My opinion is, if something is not done to arrest this evil, the consequences cannot be predicted without a shudder.

I can with the more confidence appeal to the military authorities for redress, as we have no Sheriff in this County to execute civil process.

I respectfully ask for myself and other citizens of this County that the Commander in chief, give this subject his immediate attention and afford such relief, as in his opinion our situation demands.   By permission, I refer to Lieut. Col. Sayeare for my character   I am Sir Very Respectfully Your Obedient Servant

ALS   Greer W Davis[5]

[*Endorsement*]   St Louis [*Mo.*]   Mar 7. 1863   Referred to Brig Gnl Davidson commanding District.   The matter may deserve special attention.   Slaves of loyal men should not be enticed away by our troops and our lines should not be made a fort for negroes to operate from in carrying on their contraband affairs

Beyond this I do not know that we have much to do in the premises   S R Curtis   Maj Gen[l]

> Slaves who successfully negotiated an escape to Union lines were determined to see their relatives free as well. But reconstructing families was a difficult and complex business that did not end with

the liberation of loved ones. In planning to free their kin, black men and women not only collected information about the vigilance of local slaveholders and conditions within federal territory but also prepared to support their families once they too were free. Generally, that meant waiting until they had a job—or at least had earned "a little money"—before risking the perilous journey back into the Confederacy. From the perspective of newly minted freedpeople, endangering themselves and their families for yet another form of dependence would have been a poor exchange. As superintendent of contrabands at Fortress Monroe, a federal outpost in tidewater Virginia, Captain Charles B. Wilder had seen thousands of slaves come into Union lines. His testimony before a War Department commission suggests how the slaves' desire to rebuild their family life informed the process of slavery's dissolution.

[*Fortress Monroe, Va.*]   May 9, 1863.

. . . .

Question   How many of the people called contrabands, have come under your observation?

Answer   Some 10,000 have come under our control, to be fed in part, and clothed in part, but I cannot speak accurately in regard to the number.   This is the rendezvous.   They come here from all about, from Richmond and 200 miles off in North Carolina   There was one gang that started from Richmond 23 strong and only 3 got through.

. . . .

Q   In your opinion, is there any communication between the refugees and the black men still in slavery?

A. Yes Sir, we have had men here who have gone back 200 miles.

Q   In your opinion would a change in our policy which would cause them to be treated with fairness, their wages punctually paid and employment furnished them in the army, become known and would it have any effect upon others in slavery?

A   Yes—Thousands upon Thousands.   I went to Suffolk a short time ago to enquire into the state of things there—for I found I could not get any foot hold to make things work there, through the Commanding General, and I went to the Provost Marshall and all hands—and the colored people actually sent a deputation to me one morning before I was up to know if we put black men in irons and sent them off to Cuba to be sold or set them at work and put balls on their legs and whipped them, just as in slavery; because that was the story up there, and they were frightened and didn't know what to do.   When I got at the feelings of these people I found they were not afraid of the slaveholders.   They said there was nobody on the plantations but women and they were not afraid of them   One woman came through 200 miles in Men's clothes. The most valuable information we received in regard to the Merrimack and the operations of the rebels came from the colored people and they got no credit for it.   I found hundreds who had left their wives and families behind.   I asked them "Why did you come away and leave them there?" and I found they had heard these stories, and wanted to come and see how it was.   "I am going back again after my wife" some of them have said "When I have earned a little money"   What as far as that?"   "Yes"   and I have had them come to me to borrow money, or to get their pay, if they had earned a months wages, and to get passes.   "I am going for my family" they say.   "Are you not afraid to risk it?"   "No I know the Way"   Colored men will help colored men and they will work along the by paths and get through.   In that way I have known quite a number who have gone up from time to time in the neighborhood of Richmond and several have brought back their families; some I have never heard from.   As I was saying they do not feel afraid now.   The white people have nearly all gone, the blood hounds are not there now to hunt them and they are not afraid,   before they were afraid to stir.   There are hundreds of negroes at Williamsburgh with their families working for nothing.   They would not get pay here and they had rather stay where they are.   "We are not afraid of being carried back" a great many have told us and "if we are, we can get away again"   Now that they are getting their eyes open they are coming in.   Fifty came this morning from Yorktown who followed Stoneman's Cavalry when they returned from their raid.   The officers reported to their Quartermaster that they had so many horses and fifty or sixty negroes.   "What did you bring them for"   "Why they followed us and we could not stop them."   I asked one of the men about it and he said they would leave their work in the field as soon as they found the Soldiers were Union men and follow them sometimes without hat or coat.   They would take best horse they could get and every where they rode they would take fresh horses, leave the old ones and follow on and so they came in.   I have questioned a great many of them and they do not feel much afraid; and there are a great many courageous fellows who have come from long distances in rebeldom.   Some men who came here from North Carolina, knew all about the [*Emancipation*] Proclammation and they started on the belief in it; but they had heard these stories and they wanted to know how it was.   Well, I gave them the evidence and I have no doubt their friends will hear of it.

. . . .[6]

HD

Until the Thirteenth Amendment abolished slavery throughout the nation, the door to freedom swung both ways. Men and women who escaped bondage often found themselves slapped back into slavery. This was particularly true in the slave states that had remained in the Union—Delaware, Maryland, Kentucky, and Missouri—and, as a result, were unaffected by the Emancipation Proclamation. Twelve-year-old Amy Moore and her family, who had been liberated by federal troops in northern Alabama, tried to reach the safety of the free states. But, arrested by local authorities in slaveholding Kentucky, she, her mother, and her sisters were sold back into bondage. Four months after the end of the war, when she swore this affidavit before a federal military officer, they were still held as slaves.

[*Louisville, Ky. August 14?, 1865*]

Amy Moore Colored, being duly Sworn deposeth and Says, that in the Summer of 1863 [*1862*] the United States Soldiers under command of Major McMillen came to her masters house in Huntsville Alabama, (her master and his family having left them) and carried away deponent together with her mother and three Sisters,   that they brought us all to Nashville Tenn where we were put on board of a transport and Started for Cincinnati Ohio   that when we arrived at Louisville Ky we were arrested by a man who Said he was a watchman and taken to the Slave pen on Second Street Louisville Ky and kept there two or three days when we were taken to the Depot of the Louisville and Nashville Rail Road and there another watchman took charge of us and took us to Shepherdsville Ky and kept us confined several weeks when we were sold at auction by the Sherriff of Bullett County Ky.   Dr. McKay bought deponent and paid for her the sum of Five Hundred (500) dollars   *James Funk* bought deponents mother and youngest Sister paying Six Hundred (600) dollars for the two, and Soon after Sold her mother to *Judge Hoegner* who now holds her as a Slave   *James Shepherd* bought my Sister Nora and *Richard Deets* bought my sister Ann, and further deponent saith that she and her mother and Sisters have been held as Slaves Since the above Sale and Still continue to be so held.

her

Amy ✕ Moore[7]

mark

HDSr

When slaveholders evicted slaves selectively, sending some out on their own while keeping others in bondage, they sundered families much as had the slave trade. Black people then tried to piece their families together again. The changed circumstances of freedom, especially the enlistment of black men in the Union army, provided some means of redress. But as long as the federal government honored the claims of unionist slaveholders, the former slaves' power was limited. The Union general in charge of recruiting black troops in Tennessee, a state that President Lincoln had exempted from the Emancipation Proclamation, responded to a complaint about one such case.

Memphis [*Tenn.*]   12" April 1864.

Sir: In compliance with request of Maj Genl S. A. Hurlbut made to me in communication dated Memphis Tenn 9" April 1864.

In June or July of last year 1863—Dr Wheaton a citizen living near Memphis and inside the picket lines sent two of his negro servants one man and one woman (man & wife) to the Freedmans camp with orders not to return under any circumstances—   Three Children belongig to th woman one a boy some 10 years of age and two girls 4 and 7 years of age respectivly were kept by Dr Wheaton.   For some seven months after this, neither the husband or wife saw the children.

In February last the husband, then a soldier in the US Service in Company with two other solders Colored, went to the house of Dr Wheaton situated about one half mile distant from the camp and during his absence took away the children brought them into camp and concealed them   An order was issued by Brig Genl Buckland, Comdg Dist of Memphis to the officer in command of the freedmans camp to return the children forthwith to Dr Wheaton.   After some delay the children were found and amid the tears and prostestations of the mother—were returned to Dr Wheaton where they now are.   The husband ~~and wife~~ during the past winter lived in a log house or hut and were quite comfortable

The husband is now on duty at Lake St. "Joe," Arkansas, and the wife, who has a child some six months old, is on a plantation near Goodriches Landing working for wages having been sent there by order of the officer in charge of the Freedmen of Dist of Memphis. The children are now as above stated in the custody of D[r] Wheaton and as he states held by him subject to the order of the comdg Officer Dist of Memphis. They are in good health—well clothed and well cared for generally.

The mother is charged with abusing her children at times when with D[r] Wheaton but while in Camp she is said to have conducted herself with propriety. The foregoing facts I have obtained from D[r] Wheaton— Capt Hay (who for some time past has commanded the Freedmans Camp at "Holly Springs") Mrs Hay—his wife Sergt Harrison—now on duty in Camp Holly Springs.—and others.

After carefully investigating this matter I am of the opinion that Capt Hay did not treat General Buckland's order for the return of the children with disrespect but on the contrary, used reasonable diligence in searching for the children.

It is proved that the children were not brought into the Camp immediately by the father but were concealed in the vacinity.

Capt Hay did not see the children until they were brought up and delivered to Dr Wheaton   I have the honor to be Your Obt Serv't.

HL c   *[Augustus L. Chetlain]*[8]

The dangers of trying to rescue family members still held in bondage derived not only from their owners. In the border slave states, many federal soldiers came from the slaveholding class. In addition, the state militia—with firm links to slaveowners—had little sympathy for the aspirations of former slaves. Such militia, nominally allied with the Union army, often posed as much of a threat as did the owners themselves. General Samuel R. Curtis, the federal commander in Kansas, could barely disguise his anger at the brutal abuse of one man who attempted to recover his children; he described the incident to his counterpart in Missouri.

Fort Leavenworth [Kans.],   Mar 13 *1864*

General   A negro "Sam Marshall" who resides in Leavenworth, reports to me that yesterday he went over to Platte City Missouri, to get his children, who he was told would be allowed to come away free.   The children were at a Mr Greens.   Sam went in day light, with a team, driven by a white man, and made no demonstration of insolance or disrespect to any body.   He was arrested by the Military, Commanded by one Captain David Johnson of the Mo Militia, who talked to him about the impropriety of his conduct.   The Sheriff one Jesse Morris also lectured him, and told him the Captain would send a guard to take him away, as it was a wonder he was not killed.   About a dozen of the soldiers did escort him about half a mile out of Platte City, where they tied him to a tree, and stripping him to the waste lacerated his back with a cow skin the marks of which Sam will carry to his grave.   They told him they were "introducing him to the Pawpaw Militia" and that if Col Jennison would come to Platte City, they would treat him in the same way.

The Militia were dressed in Federal uniform, and armed with revolvers

Two of them Sam knew.   They are young—"Chinn", and a young "Cockeril".

Sam is a quiet well behaved negro, whose tears and sorely lacerated back, seem to attest the truth of his statement.

The white man that drove the wagon, was arrested, but had sufficient influence (as formerly a citizen of the County) to get off without being harmed.

I call your attention to the use made of Federal troops, or troops clothed, fed, and foraged if not paid by the Federal Government.

I most respectfully suggest General, that on both sides, it is far better that troops unconnected with old border difficulties, and negro katching and negro whipping, should be substituted for such miserable wretches as those who disgrace their uniforms, and humanity, by acts of cruelty and baseness.

I hope General you will not suppose I hold you accountable for such transactions in a Command to which you have so recently been assigned; but I know a Sense of duty and disgust must be awakened by any loyal Citizen acquainted with such brutality, and I report Such matters to you, for early correction.—

They called "Sam" a Jayhawker,* and pretended that he had run off horses; but all this was no doubt a mere subterfuge; as probably the only real offense "Sam" has been guilty of, was to run himself off, with a son who has entered the Federal Army.—

Platte City, is only about 6 miles from my lines and Such treatment of men from here going into that place, is well Calculated to induce fierce resentments from this Side, which of course I shall restrain; Conscious of your own desire to correct such outrages.   I remain General Very Respectfully Yours

ALS   S. R. Curtis[9]

---

*An antislavery guerrilla operating along the Kansas-Missouri border.

The enlistment of black men in the Union army gave black people new weapons in the war against slavery. Having donned the Union blue, black soldiers believed their people were entitled to freedom, and none more so than their own kin. As the following report from a district military commander indicates, their white comrades-in-arms sometimes joined them in acting on that belief.

Warrensburg [*Mo.*]   March 29th 1864.

Colonel   I am directed by the General Commanding to state that information has been received at these Head Quarters to the effect that Negro Soldiers, on furlough from S[t] Louis with the assistance of Squads of men belonging to the command stationed at Boonville, have repeatedly crossed into Howard County and Seizing upon wagons & Teams have loaded the same with Furniture, Tobacco and such other property as they desired and bringing with them their wives & children, recrossed to this side.

The Comd[g] Officer at Boonville is said to rather encourage this unlawful proceeding as he is charged with leaving it optional with the men of his command whether they shall accompany the Negroes in their "Raids" or not.

Three such raids are said to have occurred during the first week of this Month

The General Commanding directs that you ascertain the facts and report with as little delay as possible   I have the honor to be Very Respectfully Your Ob[t] Sev[t]

James H. Steger[10]

HLcS

For fugitive slaves, the danger of recapture and the certainty of punishment were all too real. When young Jim Heiskell found himself back in his master's clutches, an older brother came to the rescue.

Slaves escaping by boat. (*Harper's Weekly,* Apr. 9, 1864)

[*Knoxville, Tenn. March 30, 1864*]

Statement of "Jim" Heiskell

My name is Jim; I have been living on Bull run, with a man by the name of Pierce; they called him Cromwell Pierce. I run off from him nearly two months ago, because he treated me so mean: he half starved and whipped me. I was whipped three or four times a week, sometimes with a cowhide, and sometimes with a hickory. He put so much work on me; I could not do it; chopping & hauling wood and lumber logs. I am about thirteen years old. I got a pretty good meal at dinner, but he only gave us a half pint of milk for breakfast and supper, with cornbread. I ran away to town; I had a brother "Bob" living in Knoxville, and other boys I knew. I would have staid on the plantation if I had been well used. I wanted also to see some pleasure in town. I hired myself to Capt. Smith as a servant, and went to work as a waiter in Quarter Master Winslow's office as a waiter for the mess. After Capt. Winslow went home, I went to live with Bob, helping him.

Last Friday just after dinner, I saw Pierce Mr. Heiskell's overseer. He caught me on Gay street, he ran after me, and carried me down Cumberland street to Mr. Heiskell's house. Mr. Heiskell, his wife and two sons, and a daughter were in the house. Mr. Heiskell asked me what made me run away; he grabbed me by the back of the ears, and jerked me down on the floor on my face; Mr. Pierce held me & Mr. Heiskell put irons on my legs. Mr. Heiskell took me by the hair of my head, and Mr. Pierce took me around my body, they carried me upstairs, and then Mr. Heiskell dagged me into a room by my hair. They made me stand up, and then they laid me down on my belly & pulled off my breeches as far as they could, and turned my shirt and jacket up over my head. (I heard Mr Heiskell ask for the cowhide before he started with me upstairs.) Mr. Pierce held my legs, and Mr. Heiskell got a straddle of me, and whipped me with the rawhide on my back & legs. Mr. Pierce is a large man, and very strong. Mr. Heiskell rested two or three times, and begun again. I hollowed—"O, Lord" all the time. They whipped me, it seemed to me, half an hour. They then told me to get up and dress, and said if I did'nt behave myself up there they would come up again and whip me again at night. The irons were left on my legs. Mr. Heiskell came up at dark and asked me what that "yallow nigger was talking to me about". He meant my brother Bob, who had been talking to me opposite the house. I was standing up and when he (Mr. Heiskell) asked me about the "yaller nigger", he kicked me with his right foot on my hip and knocked me over on the floor, as the irons were on my feet, I could not catch myself. I knew my brother Bob was around the house trying to get me out. About one hour by sun two soldiers came to the house, one staid & the other went away. I saw them through the window. They had sabres. I thought they had come to guard me to keep Bob from getting me. I heard Bob whisling, and I went to the window and looked through the curtain. Bob told me to hoist the window, put something under it & swing out of the window. I did as my brother told me, and hung by my hands. Bob said "Drop," but I said I was afraid I would hurt myself. Bob said "Wait a minute and I will get a ladder". He brought a ladder and put it against the house, under the window. I got halfway down before they hoisted the window; I fell & Bob caught me and run off with me in his arms. I saw Mr. Pierce sitting at the window, he had a double-barreled gun in his hands. By the time I could count three I heard a gun fired two or three times, quick, I heard Mr. Pierce call "Jim" "Jim" and the guards hollered "halt; halt!" I had no hat or shoes on. We both hid, and laid flat on the ground. I saw the guard, running around there hunting for us. After lying there until the guards had gone away, we got up and Bob carried me to a friend's house. I had the irons on my legs. I got some supper and staid there until next day.   My irons were taken off by a colored man, who carried me to the hospital.   I am now employed working in the hospital N$^{\circ}$ 1.

                                              his

—signed— Jim ✕ Heiskell—[11]

                                             mark

> Former slaves sometimes called on others for assistance in rescuing their families. Three freedmen employed as military laborers in the District of Columbia hired two white teamsters with whom they had worked to take them to southern Maryland to liberate their wives and children. The group moved quickly, located the families, and were returning to Washington when they were arrested and imprisoned by civil authorities in Maryland. The wife of one of the teamsters appealed to the War Department for her husband's release, and an endorsement by a Union general described the circumstances of the case.

                             Washington City [*D.C.*]   May 25th 1864

Mrs Laura A. Moody, of Washington, D.C., applies for the release of her husband Geo. A. Moody, who while attempting to bring from Piscataway, Md some negro women to their husbands, living in this city under Government employ, was arrested and imprisoned in Lower Marlboro Jail.   Mr Moody had a pass and had been informed he would not be interfered with, or if he was so interfered with that he would be protected by Government[12]

[*Endorsement*]   Hd. Qrs. First Separate Brigade   Relay House [*Md.*] June 1" 64.   Respectfully returned to Depm't. Hd. Qrs. with the information that Detective Wm W. Wood was intrusted with the investigation of this case and reports that Geo A. Moody and a Mr. Jones, were employed by three (3) Negro's (contrabands then in the employ of the U. S. Govm't) to go to Piscataway after the wives and children of these contrabands, who accompanied Moody and Jones on papers purporting to be issued by Cap't Shutz Provost Marshal.   In the execution of what they supposed to be authorized by these papers, they, collected the women & children and were on their way to Washington with them, when they were arrested by a Constable, by the name of Kirby (Jones and one colored man eluding the officer) who took Moody, two of the negro men with the women and children before Dr. G. [F]. Harris a justice of the Peace, who ordered them committed to jail.   Subsequently Jones who had returned to Washington, at the solicitation of Moody's wife accompanied her to Upper Marlboro Jail to see her husband; On their arrival, Jones was arrested and confined in Jail with Moody.

It appears that Moody and Jones were employed by these colored men because of their having a wagon and horses with which to transport their women and children, and having made their acquaintance while engaged upon the same work for the Govm't near Washington.   It appears further that these men (Moody & Jones) are very poor and ignorant, and their families dependent entirely upon their efforts for daily subsistence   being brothers in law, they had obtained a team and wagon with which they performed such jobs as they could get from the Govm't and private parties who might require their service.

Being employed occasionally at the [Correll] where these Negroes were at work, and being offered a paying price for this job, they undertook it and fell into the hands of the *Phillistines.*

Their ignorance and utter destitution [. . .]* idea of any intention to

---

*Approximately two words obscured by an ink blot.

commit a crime [. . .] [with] them a Provost Marshals pass would be regarded a passport to the realms of eternal bliss if it was so written.   In as much as they supposed they were acting under the authority of proper Military Power, I would recommend if it can be done, that their cases be investigated by a Military commission   E. B. Tyler—Brig Genl:

> Further investigation revealed that Moody, Jones, and the two black men had become objects of spite among local slaveholders. Transferred from Prince George's County, where they had been captured, to the jail in Charles County, they were "heavily chained to the floor with fetters upon their feet" and "handcuffed together at night." On June 24, the Secretary of War instructed the federal commander in Maryland to secure their release.[13]

> Perhaps recognizing the risk of acting on his own and the futility of applying to civil authorities, a former slave from Maryland asked the Secretary of War to help him reunite his family.

Boston [*Mass.*]   July 26th 1864

Dear Sir   I am Glad that I have the Honour to Write you afew line   I have been in troble for about four yars   my Dear wife was taken from me Nov 19th 1859 and left me with three Children and I being a Slave At the time Could Not do Anny thing for the poor little Children for my master it was took me Carry me some forty mile from them So I Could Not do for them and the man that they live with half feed them and half Cloth them & beat them like dogs & when I was admited to go to see them it use to brake my heart & Now I say agian I am Glad to have the honour to write to you to see if you Can Do Anny thing for me or for my poor little Children   I was keap in Slavy untell last Novr 1863. then the Good lord sent the Cornel borne [*William Birney?*] Down their in Marland in worsester Co   So as I have been recently freed I have but letle to live on but I am Striveing Dear Sir   but what I went too know of you Sir is is it possible for me to go & take my Children from those men that keep them in Savery   if it is possible will you pleas give me a permit from your hand then I think they would let them go   I Do Not know what better to Do but I am sure that you know what is best for me to Do

my two son I left with Mr Josep Ennese & my litle daughter I left with Mr Iven Spence in worsister Co [. . .] of Snow hill

Hon sir will you please excuse my Miserable writeing & answer me as soon as you can   I want get the little Children out of Slavery, I being Criple would like to know of you also if I Cant be permited to rase a Shool Down there & on what turm I Could be admited to Do so   No more At present Dear Hon Sir

John Q A Dennis

Hon Sir will you please direct your letter to No 4 1/2 Milton St Boston mass[14]

ALS

> There is no indication that the War Department so much as acknowledged Dennis's letter.

———•———

> If high-ranking federal officials only occasionally responded to the petitions of former slaves, freedpeople sometimes received assistance from less exalted quarters. Like former slaves in many parts

of the Union-occupied South, a group of military laborers in eastern Virginia returned home to liberate their families. They were
accompanied by a detachment of black soldiers, whose brigade
commander reported the outcome of the dangerous expedition.

Newport-News, Va. Sept. 1st, 1864.

Sir, I have the honor to report that some Government employees (colored) came up here from Fort Monroe and Hampton Hospitals, having
been allowed a short leave of absence for the purpose of getting their
families if possible. I told them I had no boats, but would help them
with men. They reappeared the next day with sailboats. I sent with
them a Captain and 15 men (dismounted Cavalry). The families were
in and about Smithfield. I gave them strict instructions to abstain from
plundering—to injure no one if possible—to get the women and children
merely, and come away as promptly as possible. They were to land in
the night. They followed these directions closely: but became delayed
by the numbers of women and children anxious to follow, whom they
packed in extra boats, picked up there, and towed along. They also had
to contend against a head tide, and wind calm. So that their progress
down Smithfield Creek in the early morn was exceedingly slow. The
inhabitants evidently gathered in from some concerted plan of alarm or
signals. For, 3 miles below, the party were intercepted by a force of
irregular appearance, numbering about 100—having horses and dogs
with them;—armed variously with shot guns, rifles, &c, and posted
behind old breastworks with some hurried additions. They attacked the
leading boats, killed a man and woman, and wounded another woman
therein. The contrabands then rowed over to the opposite bank and
scattered over the marshes. How many more have been slaughtered we
know not. Two (2) men have since escaped to us singly.— When the

rear boats, containing the soldiers, came up, the Captain landed, with the design of attacking the rebels. But then the firing revealed their full numbers. He found they outnumbered him, more than 6 to 1, and that the REVOLVERS of our Cavalry, in open boats or on the open beach, would stand no chance against their rifles behind breastworks. He embarked again, and they made their way past the danger, by wading his men behind the boats, having the baggage and bedding piled up like a barricade. They then had a race with 3 boats, which put out from side creeks to cut them off. But for the coolness and ingenuity of Capt. Whiteman, none would have escaped. None of the soldiers are known to have been severely wounded; but 3 are missing in the marshes and woods.

. . . .

HLS   Edw[d] A. Wild[15]

> Having played their part in the Union's success, black soldiers con-
> sidered themselves entitled to assistance in securing their families'
> freedom. A black sergeant stationed in Florida felt confident that
> the general who had supervised recruitment in his home state
> would bestow "a Small favor."

Barrancas Fla. Dec 27. 1864

Sir   I beg you the granterfurction of a Small favor   will you ples to Cross the Mississippia River at Bayou Sar La. with your Command & jest on the hill one mile from the little town you will finde A plantation Called Mrs Marther. H. Turnbuill & take a way my Farther & mother & my brothers wife with all their Childern & U take them up at your He[d] Quarters. & write to me   Sir the ar ther & I will amejeately Send after

Letter from Sergeant Joseph J. Harris to General Daniel Ullman. (See pp. 49–50) them. I wishes the Childern all in School. it is beter for them then to be their Surveing a mistes. Sir it isent mor then three or four Hours trubel   I have bain trying evry sence I have bin in the servis it is goin on ner 3. years & Could never get no one to so do for me   now I thinks it will be don for you is my Gen. I wishes evry day you would send after us. our Regt. ar doing all the hard fightin her   we have disapointe the Rebes & surprizeed theme in all. importan pointes   they says they wishes to Captuer the 82nd Regt that they woul murdar them all   they Calls our Reg^t the Bluebellied Eagles   Sir my Farthers Name Adam Harris   he will Call them all to gether. & tel him to take Cousan Janes Childarn with hime

Joseph. J. Harris

Sir I will remain Ob your Soldiar in the U. S. A.[16]
ALS

Even after the war came to an end, black people had difficulty reconstructing their families. Those in Kentucky faced particular difficulties, for slavery remained legal there until December 1865, when the Thirteenth Amendment was ratified. The families of black soldiers, however, were entitled to freedom under a joint resolution of Congress.* Acting under its provisions and armed with an order from the federal commander in Kentucky, a sergeant on furlough from his regiment attempted to remove his family from their owner's control, only to find himself clapped into jail. His company commander recounted the episode to the regimental commander, who added his own endorsement.

---

*Adopted on March 3, 1865, the joint resolution freed the wives and children of black soldiers, regardless of their owners' loyalty. (*Statutes at Large*, vol. 13, p. 571.)

Battery Rodgers, Va— November 15th 1865—

Sir: I have the honor to make the following statement, relating to Serg't Tho[s] M[c]Dougal of Co. "F" 107th U.S.C.I. who received a Furlough of thirty days on the 1st of October 1865, to visit his family in Ky.; and would respectfully request that it be forwarded to the proper authorities in order that *justice* may be done in his case.

After reaching Louisville Ky. Serg't M[c]Dougal got an order from Gen'l Palmer,—in charge of the Freedman's Bureau of Kentucky,—to move his family to Louisville— His wife is living with her old master Hillary Johnson, Judge of the county of Larue Ky, and living in the town of Hodgensville. he is an old rebel and one of some note in that County.— Serg't M[c]Dougal was arrested by Johnson soon after reaching Hodgensville, his order taken from him and he lodged in the County jail, where he has been confined since October 24th 1865, on account of trying to free his family from bondage.

The above is a true statement of the case at it has reached me.

Serg't M[c]Dougal is a superior Non-com. Officer and his services are much needed in this Company. I am sir, very respectfully, Your obedient servant,

ALS   F. B. Clark[17]

[*Endorsement*] Hd Qrs 107th U.S. C[*olored*] Inf'y Fort Corcoran V[a]. Nov 21st 1865 Respectfully forwarded. Quite a number of instances have occurred where men of this Regiment have been incarcerated in prison upon the most frivolous pretences. The Regiment was organized in Kentucky; and when the men return home to provide for their families they are often shamefully treated by their former masters. Especially is such the case in the interior districts of the state, where the disloyal element strongly preponderates, and where it is impossible for colored soldiers to obtain justice from magistrates who despise the Federal

uniform—particularly so when worn by their former slaves. I would
respectfully request that some action be taken to have Sergt McDougall
released, so that he can return to his regt as soon as practicable   D. M.
Sells. Lt. Co^l. Comdg

> Forwarded through military channels, Captain Clark's letter even-
> tually reached General Palmer, in Kentucky, who endorsed it as
> follows.

Louisville [*Ky.*]   Nov 30 1865

   Respectfully returned to Col C W Foster A[*ssistant*] A[*djutant*]
G[*eneral*] with the remark that the case of Sergeant McDougal
illustrates in an eminent degree the peculiar ideas of loyalty honesty,
and justice which animates certain of the judicial officers of Kentucky
The facts as I have ascertained them are substantially as follows.
McDougal went to the house of Johnson who is county Judge of Larue
County Ky and formerly owned McDougals wife and demanded
her   Johnson refused to give her up without my order which was
promptly given   He then removed his family from Johnsons house and
in doing so inadvertently took with them the clothes of some other
colored child of the value of 75. cts as I am advised   When these
clothes were demanded of him he said "There they are take them   I
knew nothing about them supposed they belonged to my children" which
I am assured by respectable people is true.   Judge Johnson however
had him arrested for larceny brought before himself and committed him
to jail in default of bail   (The Judge it is reported takes the astute
distinction that though the act of Congress may free the wives and
children of soldiers "it does not divest the owner of the title to the

clothes they wear")   I at once took steps to investigate the case found the facts as before stated with the additional fact that a loyal man had become McDougals bail and the court just at hand   As the soldier was in civil custody upon colorable process authorised for a scandalous purpose in a rascally way I determined to wait the action of the Court trusting that justice would be done   The court met on last Monday— The result of its action will be promptly reported

I may add that the colored soldiers who return to this state are persecuted and outraged in many ways.

<small>AES</small>   John M Palmer[18]

In January 1866, General Palmer reported that the grand jury had failed to indict McDougal, who was reunited with his family.[19]

Former slaves at Cumberland Landing, Virginia. (Library of Congress)

CHAPTER

FAMILIES IN
THE UNION-OCCUPIED
CONFEDERACY

AS UNION TROOPS PENETRATED THE CONFED-
eracy, the opportunities for slaves to escape bondage and
place their family life on a firm foundation increased. For more and
more slaves, federal encampments were no longer remote sites
from which they were separated by the Confederate army but a
nearby town or meadow where Union troops bivouacked. Occasionally, federal troops marched right by the plantation doorstep and
slaves merely tagged behind the long blue line. If fugitive slaves
continued to face difficulties in areas like Tennessee and southern
Louisiana, which President Lincoln exempted from the Emancipation Proclamation, and in other places where federal officers
catered to slaveholders who claimed to be unionists, nothing could
prevent the deterioration of slavery once the Union army arrived.
The number of fugitives shot upward, and the work of family
reconstruction proceeded apace.

Slave flight became a family affair. As federal forces drew near,
the fugitive population, which early in the war comprised predomi-
nantly young men, increasingly included women, children, and

older people, as families fled en masse. Unwilling to abandon their loved ones to the mercy of vengeful owners, fugitive slaves often moved from plantation to plantation reassembling kin networks that had been divided for years. The business of flight and family reconstitution became one and the same as the possibilities of successful escape grew.

Federal officers, even those who valued the labor of black men and women, were of two minds about the exodus. While they welcomed the fugitives as a loss to the Confederacy and a gain for the Union, they worried about the expense, inconvenience, and confusion that accompanied the destruction of chattel bondage. Fugitive-slave families jammed roads and obstructed military operations. The wives, children, and parents of newly enlisted black men often huddled on the outskirts of federal encampments. To prevent massive destitution and epidemic disease, the soldiers' relatives and other fugitive slaves required logistical support in the form of food, clothing, and medicine, and men who left their families to enlist or to work as military laborers fully expected the federal government to provide it. Not all Union officers shared this expectation, and some were actively hostile to the freedpeople's desire to reconstruct their domestic life, especially when the reconstituted families seemed to impede the army's military mission.

Freedpeople, however, had friends who shared their goals. Scores of concerned northerners—many of them with abolitionist pedigrees—came south to minister to the needs of former slaves. Some did so under the auspices of freedmen's aid societies or other philanthropic groups; others could be found within the ranks of the Union army, especially among the chaplains and medical officers. While former slaves welcomed the food, clothing, and medicine distributed by such men and women, they often found that the northerners' notions about appropriate family arrangements differed from their own. The freedpeople's struggle to remake their families was thus complicated by the intervention of friends as well as foes.

In southern Louisiana, where many slaveholders claimed to be loyal to the Union, the exemption from the Emancipation Proclamation put black soldiers' families constantly at risk. An anonymous white unionist informed the local federal commander of a kidnapping ring that was forcing soldiers' families back into bondage.

New Orleans [*La.*],   Apil 3[d] 1863.

Dear Gen[l],   the writer of this beg leave to State the following facts. which can be proved. by overwhelming testimony.

George Johnson. alias Merritt. is a regularly enlisted man, in Company B. Captain. W[m] B. Barrett. 2[d] Regiment Native Guards. La Vols. and has a family consisting of wife and three children.

Recently four whitemen, pretending to be acting under authority of Capt Sawyer. Provost Marshall of St Bernard. came to the residence of the wife of George Johnson. N° 90 Circus St. and kidnapped her. carried her down to the plantation of Dr T. B. Merritt. Eleven miles down the Mexican Gulf Rail Road. and there subjected her to the most cruel and unmerciful treatment.   the Overseer of the plantation. whose name is Stamply. beat her unmercifully with a Stick.   he afterward turned her clothes over her head, and Struck fifty two lashes.   at the time he was thus punishing her. the Driver. remarked. M[r] Stamply. if you dont be careful. you will Kill that woman.   thereupon, Stamply drew his Revolver. and pointing it at the Driver; Said, God damn you, if you Say another word. I'll blow your brains out.   the Yankee's have turned all you Niggers fools. and I intend to Kill all the niggers I can. and it will not be long. before all the Yankee's in Louisiana were killed off. and those who were not Killed. would have to run off.

On last Sunday. March 29th 1863. Dr's Merritt. and Knapp. and Maj. Walker. met at a Station on the Mex. Gulf. R.R. and had with them the woman before mentioned. who had been previously brought there in the cars. they proceeded down the road to the plantation of one Ducrow. they then and there whipped her unmercifully and cruelly, for the purpose of making her tell where the other negroes were. and to give up her Ration certificate, which they called. 'Damned Yankee Documents'   as to the documents, she could not give them up, as they were in this city. as to the negroes. she Knew nothing of their whereabouts. her name is Arana Johnson, This woman is the property of a man named Patton. a Rebel. now at Vicksburg, he was one of those who fired into the fleet. as it came up the River. last April, Patton is also married to a Daughter of Dr Merritt,

There is concealed. Somewhere in the vicinity of the plantations of these gentlemen, a large quantity of Medicine, which they intend to Smuggler to the Rebels. the woman Knows where it is concealed. and will show the proper authorities the Spot. She is now at Dr Merritt. Plantation. they having found out. that further concealment would not do.

General, if you will investigate this matter, it will be of no use to apply to Capt Sawyer. the Provost Marshall. down there. as he is in league with the planters. and, tell them to treat the negroes as they please that he will take good care to see that nothing Shall be known at headquarters, and especially of this case. of pesecuting the wife of a United States Soldier.

Capt. Sawyer is Selling Soldier rations to the planters down there.

It is but recently that an old man was starved to death. by being confined in the Stocks. and allowed nothing to eat. from which he died.

There are a great many union persons down there. who all say that it is a Shame that this woman Should thus be persecuted. and that if it were known at head quarters. it would not be allowed to exist.

I am heart. head. and hand for the union. and hope to see it shortly put down this Rebellion and with it the vile and wicked institution of Slavery.   Knowing the facts here in Stated, my own feeling will not Suffer me to remain Silent. that the proper remedy. may be applied. feeling that if Known at head quarters the parties offending may brought to

HLSr   *Justice*[1]

> As the organization of black regiments expanded throughout the Mississippi Valley, tens of thousands of black men took up arms for the Union. Their families often gathered on the outskirts of the regimental camps, where they could maintain contact with husbands and fathers and gain protection from marauding bands of Confederate guerrillas. At first federal authorities made little provision for the women, children, and old people, who, as a result, suffered from disease and neglect. Forced upon their own resources, the "contrabands" drew on connections of kin and community to create new lives in difficult circumstances. A medical officer assigned to inspect the condition of black troops in northeastern Louisiana added to his report some observations about the former slaves living in what he termed "contraband family camps."

Vicksburg [*Miss.*]   July 27th 1863

Sir: Learning that you take great interest in the organization and general condition of the negro regiments now organizing in this and other Departments, and having been appointed to inspect these regiments from Lake Providence to Sherman's Landing, I take the liberty of sending you a copy of my report of the above inspection.

In the same district I found about ten thousand women and children, who, having left their plantations, were roving about without adequate support or protection.   My report on the condition of these contrabands,

forms the conclusion of this report.   Respectfully Your Obedient
Servant

James Bryan

Report.

The ground indicated is about eighty miles in extent, on the right
bank of the Mississippi, stretching up the river from Vicksburg.   Like
the banks of this stream generally, the ground is flat, and in some places
wet, the overflow of the river being guarded by a single or double
levee.   The exact points occupied by the negro regiments, counting from
above, are Goodrich's Landing, about ten miles below Lake Providence,
and Milliken's Bend, ten miles above Young's Point.   Outside of these
encampments, however, are numerous contraband family camps, which
extend along the shore down to Sherman's Landing.   It does not come
within the province of the letter of the order, to report upon the
contrabands, but I have understood that the Medical Director is
desirous that the inspection should extend also to them.

.   .   .   .

Contrabands.

I shall speak of the contrabands, as distinct from the soldiers, in the
following particulars.

First.   They are the families of soldiers and others, and consist of
women, children, and worn out old men.   The women and children are
profitable to the slave dealer.   It is said, for instance, that some of the
quasi agents of the government, have an understanding with the
guerillas to supply them with negroes at the following rates.   A male
$300, a female $200, a likely child $100.   Some of those agents, it is
said, in times of raids, are found leading the rebels to their spoils.

The greater number of contrabands, however, are necessarily
children, who suffer very much from exposure and want of proper
protection.

Second.   Many of the children are capable of moderate employment, which would support them well.   The mothers also, and other young and middle aged women, are most of them vigorous and able, if properly employed, to support themselves comfortably with their young children. The aged blacks, broken down by years and toil, are still able, during the short period of their existence, to do light work of some kind.   I am informed that the most successful and wealthy planters, allow no old persons to be entirely idle, but keep them occupied at such light work as may be suitable to their years or strength.   Occasionally I found one of these who knew how to read, whose talents might be well employed in teaching the younger children the elements of an education.   Their burials and other religious services, conducted chiefly by these old patriarchs, are very impressive and calculated to sustain the religious tone of the race.   The diseases found amongst the children, are very much the same as those seen among the children of the poor in the large cities of the North.   Their mortality in this wandering life, appears to be very great, and the affectionate mother weeps over the dying babe with the sad reflection that a few simple medicines, with the comforts of life, would have been sufficient to prolong its existence.   They are more independent in their habits than many suppose.   Their own "grannies", who are generally youngish or middle aged mulatto women, are well skilled in most of the simple and many of the scientific medical agents of our art.   These "grannies" are an institution fostered by the economical planter.   He selects an intelligent young woman, places her under the special guidance and instruction of the plantation Doctor, who carefully teaches her the effects and doses of medicines, which she administers to the sick during his absence.   These "grannies" are found among the contrabands not unfrequently, and if well supplied by the government with medicines, would do great good with them.   The great number of children and old persons in these camps, give them much the character of a hospital, and I would suggest that the government, in addition to securing the services of these grannies, appoint medical men, in the ratio of one to three thousand, to distribute medicine and prescribe for the sick. The Surgeon might also draw rations in the absence of other officers, and see that his patients are properly fed. There is not, in my opinion, any necessity for the establishment of a hospital for this class of people; they are bound together by family ties and will not willingly be separated. These attachments are not easily broken. In times of sickness and distress, they prefer assisting their relatives, to neighbors or strangers.

Finally. As the arrangements for the contrabands in their present unsettled condition, must necessarily be temporary, I have only the two suggestions above named to make. The final distribution of these laborers, and their employment in different avocations of life as free men and free women, must be left to the wisdom and power of that great Government, which, now, with outstretched arms, breaks the shackles of their long enduring slavery, and bids a nation of four millions of people, be forever free.

One suggestion, however, I would add; it is that the children be immediately instructed in the elements of an English education. Large numbers of elementary books, primers, spelling books &c, should be distributed among them, and good white teachers be employed by government to instruct all the black children within the Federal lines. All of which is respectfully submitted.[2]

ALcS

> Federal supervision of labor arrangements in occupied territory
> allowed some husbands and wives who had been separated under
> slavery to take up residence on the same plantation. In the spring

of 1863, Ruben Win moved to the plantation where his wife, Marcelline, was employed. He expected more from freedom, however, than simple proximity to his wife. When the overseer abused her, Win entered a complaint that brought upon himself the wrath of the infuriated overseer; his father-in-law received a similar response when he, too, objected to his daughter's treatment.

[*Terrebonne Parish, La.*]   21st day of November 1863

Ruben Win colored sworn according to law deposes and says, that he lives on the Quitman plantation on grand Caillou parish of Terrebonne that on Thursday last the overseer of said plantation Mr Bauvais reproved his wife Marcelline who is far avanced in the family way, about her work, and when she said that it was not her who cut the stubble to high, said Bauvais got down from his horse and struck her with a cane some ten times, and that afterwards he struck her with the handle of a cane knife over the head some five or six times,   that his wife went off [. . .]* to him said deponant, who was about fifty yards from her,   that said Bauvais, who had got on his horse, rode over her, making her fall down,   that deponant went to Mr Pelton, who is agent of the plantation. to complain to him about the bad treatment of his wife—   that Mr Pelton said that it was not right for the overseer to illtreat his wife.   that when deponant came back the same evening to the plantation, and had told the overseer that he had complained to Mr Pelton, said Bauvais first struck him in the [face] with his fist, and then struck him with his gun violently on the stomach twice,   said Bauvais then had his gun cocked,   he had also a pistol with him

his

Ruben × Win

mark

---

*Two illegible words.

Henry White colored sworn says that he is the father of the negro woman Marcelline, that on the evening when Mr Beauvais had been beating Marcelline he spoke to her, examined her wrist, which was swollen. and told her to go to her cabin. that he would see next day if Mr Bauvais had the right to beat the people on the place. that then Mr Bauvais struck him with his fist on the stomach and knocked him down

his

Henry × White[3]

mark

HDSr

No inequity of military life was as galling to black soldiers as the federal government's refusal to pay them the same wages white soldiers received. More was at stake than their dignity or even justice itself. As the commander of one black regiment reported to departmental headquarters, inadequate pay and the demands of military duty prevented black soldiers from fulfilling their responsibilities to their families.

Camp Bennett   Hilton Head SC   November 30" 1863.
Captain   I have the honor most Respectfully to request that the families of men of 3^d S.C. Infty be furnished with rations until such time as their pay will be raised and enable them to furnish means for their support.   In making this request I would respectfully call the attention of the General Comdg^s to the following facts.

On the Organization of this regiment the families of the men, received rations by Genl D. Hunter's orders,*   those rations have from time to

---

*General Order 17, issued on March 6, 1863, by General David Hunter, then the federal commander in coastal South Carolina, had called for a draft of all able-bodied black men between the

time been curtailed, and now they are entirely taken away,   some of the men have large families unable to procure sufficient food and are in a deplorable condition.— The pay of the men being only seven dollars ($7) per month, and being obliged to remain in Camp to attend to their military duty they are unable to render the least assistance towards the support of those who are depended upon them; while Colored men employed in the *Quartermaster's* Department receive from 10 to 25 dollars per month, with ample opportunity for the cultivation of the soil, do receive full rations for their families thereby causing great dissatisfaction among the men of this Command   Hoping that the above will meet with the approval of the General Comdg.   I am Capt Very Respectfully Your most Ob^t Ser^t

HLS   Aug's. G. Bennett[4]

> When the department commander directed that "application for subsistence stores should be made to [military governor] Brig. Gen'l Rufus Saxton," Saxton responded that "a habit of dependence upon the government for food and clothing ought to be discouraged among the freedmen, even at the risk of some suffering"; accordingly, rations would be issued "only to those in extreme destitution, unable to help themselves, and having no relatives who can support them."[5]

ages of eighteen and fifty. A portion of the order had stated that "[u]ntil other arrangements can be made, the families of all negroes thus drafted will be provided for by orders which General Saxton has authority to issue." Hunter had added, however, the following qualification: "[I]t is hoped and confidently believed that, in the present scarcity of labor . . . few such families will be thrown upon the Government for support." (*Official Records*, ser. 1, vol. 14, pp. 1020–21.)

Former slaves planting sweet potatoes on Edisto Island, South Carolina. (New-York Historical Society)

When left to their own devices, former slaves reconstituted their families as best they could. In northern Virginia, on the outskirts of the nation's capital, a group of sixteen families established a small settlement, with the men working as laborers in nearby military depots and the women tending the children and keeping house in the shanties they proudly called home. The wife of an army chaplain described how their efforts came to naught when the federal government unaccountably changed its policy respecting the settlement.

[*Washington, D.C.?   January? 1864*]

Mrs Louisa Jane Barker (wife of Chaplain Barker (1st Mass Heavy Artillery

I know the spot of ground which was assigned by Lieut Shepard to the colord people to build their cottages upon.   A little village had collected there.   I made frequent visits among them to ascertain their wants, plans occupations &c   Their freedom had been taken mostly under the Presidents [*Emancipation*] proclamation of January 1st 1863   Since that time they had not only supported themselves, and their families, but saved money enough to build the little shanties they then occupied They expressed great reluctance to enter the contraband camp, because they felt more independent in supporting themselves, and families, after the manner of white laborers.

I think they were proud of their past success—   The first help they required was education—   Every head of a family eagerly entered into my proposition to start a school for their children   They gave their names to be responsible for tuition at any rate I might decide upon to be paid monthly—   A well educated mulatto woman engaged to take the school as soon as a building could be procured   I interested some gentlemen of Boston in my plan, and had obtained the promise of a

contribution of a part, if not the whole of a school house, when the whole
project was thwarted by a sudden order for a second removal of this
village outside of the Rifle pits or into the Contraband Camp. This
order created great unhappiness amongst them—

I enquired of the most intelligent negro whether any complaint had
been made to him as to the new settlement— He had not heard of any
just ground of complaint from any one— several groundless
complaints had been mad: there was no truth in them.

About ten days after this conversation a body of soldiers entered the
village claiming to have been sent by Genl Augur with peremptory
orders "to clear out this village." This order was executed so literally
that even a dying child was ordered out of the house— The
grandmother who had taken care of it since its mothers death begged
leave to stay until the child died, but she was refused

The men who were absent at work, came home at night to find empty
houses, and their families gone, they knew not whither!— Some of
them came to Lieut Shepard to enquire for their lost wives and
children—

In tears and indignation they protested against a tyranny worse than
their past experiences of slavery— One man said "I am going back to
my old master— I never saw hard times till since I called myself a
freeman—

I have never seen any of the sixteen families composing this
settlement since the conversation above alluded to; and I regret to find
that I have lost the list of their names—[6]

HD

Once committed to the use of black soldiers, federal officials often
failed to draw the line at voluntary enlistment. In parts of the
Union-occupied Confederacy, particularly tidewater Virginia and

North Carolina, impressment became the order of the day. As a result, the arrival of federal soldiers that signaled for some black people the chance to reconstitute family life marked for others the disruption and sometimes the destruction of established households. Jane Wallis, the wife of a shoemaker, protested the seizure of her husband.

[*York Co., Va.   December 10, 1863*]

Sir   I take the liberty to pen you a few lines, stating my own case,   the Soldiers have taken my Husband away, from me, on yesterday, and it was against his will, and he is not competent to bee A Soldier.   he is verry delicate, and in bad health, in the Bargin, and I am not healthy myself, but if they, keep him, they leave me, and 3 children, to get along, the best we can, and one of them is now verry Sick.   do try and get them to release him if you can, for they too[k] him, when he was on his way to his work.   he is A shoo make by trade,   his Name is James Wallis. pleas do all you can

ALS   Jane Wallis, his wife[7]

The Union army frequently impressed black soldiers with an efficiency that left no room for familial responsibilities. Occasionally, a sympathetic officer might allow an impressed man to return home to inform loved ones of his fate, but manpower needs generally overruled compassion.

[*Craney Island, Va.*]   Jan. 2nd 1864

Statement of John Banks (Colored) in the matter of recruiting colored men, by force.

My name is John Banks, am about 24 years of age, live at the Parrish Farm, one mile this side of Newport News where I have a mother & wife.

On the 2^d day of Dec. 1863 I was cutting wood in the woods about a mile from my house when a number of colored soldiers, armed (probably about ten men) came upon me and asked me to enlist. I told them that I could not enlist because I was obliged to do the work for my family. They then obliged me to go to Newport News to see Capt. Montgomery, their Commanding Officer. I begged Capt. Montgomery to release me or at least to let me go home to see my family. He treated me kindly and let me go home under guard & stay about five minutes. He said he couldnt release me because he "had *orders*" to take all colored men & make them enlist, but that he would send me to Col. Nelson at Craney Island & if I didn't wish to remain the Col. would send me home the next morning. I was then sent the same day to Craney Island on a tug, surrounded by armed soldiers, just as though I was a prisoner.

Arriving at Craney Island I heard such stories of men being obliged to "tote" balls because they refused to enlist and also of their being confined in the guard house on hard bread & water, that when my enlistment papers were made out I did not dare to remonstrate but accepted the five dollars bounty and my uniform and clothing and performed the duty of a soldier. I was detailed for duty in the Quartermaster's Dept. at Norfolk five days, part of which time I was under guard, so that I could not even go to get a drink of water without an armed soldier going with me.

While at Newport News a soldier told George Marrow and me that if we didn't enlist he would put the contents of his musket into us.

At Craney Island I saw Bob Smith put into the guard house because he would not enlist.[8]

HD

The army needed laborers as well as soldiers and, when volunteers could not be found, federal authorities seldom hesitated to seize black men and assign them to labor far from their families. Impressment not only separated men from their wives, children, and other kin, but it also subverted the economic foundation on which a stable family life rested. When former slaves who had not yet been paid for their work on federal fortifications in coastal North Carolina were indiscriminately impressed and sent to another such assignment in Virginia, their ability to sustain their families faltered. Declaring themselves committed to the Union's success and willing to work for it, forty-five freedmen petitioned the commander of federal forces in tidewater Virginia and North Carolina for their families to be assured basic sustenance.

Bermuda Hundred's V.A.   Septm 1864

Sir,   you will pardon us for troubling you with this report, but knowing you to be a Gentleman of Justice and a friend to the Negro race in this country, we take the liberty to send you the following facts.

Forty five of us Colored people, worked for four months throughing up breast work's at Roanoke Island.   Augt 31st we were told to report at head quarters to be paid.   we went according to orders.   when we got there, a guard of soldiers was put over us, and we marched on board a steamer, at the point of the bayonet.   we were told the paymaster was on board the steamer, to pay us, then we was to go to Fortress Munroe. then told that we was going to Dutch Gap to be paid.   true we was on the way to Dutch Gap to work on the canal.

guards were then sent over the Island to take up every man that could be found indiscriminately young and old sick and well.   the soldiers broke into the couloured people's house's taken sick men out of bed.   men that had sick wives, and men that had large family's of children and no wife or person to cut wood for them or take care of them, were taken, and not asked one question or word about going,   had we been asked to go to dutch gap a large number would have gone without causeing the suffering that has been caused,   we are willing to go where our labour is wanted and we are ready at any time to do all we can for the goverment at any place and feel it our duty to help the goverment all we can, but goverment dont know the treatment we receive from Sup^{t}s of contrabands.

   we have not been paid for our work don at Roanoke, consequently our wives and family's are there suffering for clothes.   Captn James has paid us for only two months work this year, the month's of Febuary and January.   No one knows the injustice practiced on the negro's at Roanoke,   our garden's are plundere'd by the white soldiers.   what we raise to surport ourselves with is stolen from us, and if we say any thing about it we are sent to the guard house.   rations that the goverment allows the contrabands are sold to the white secech citizen's, and got out the way at night.   its no uncommon thing to see weman and children crying for something to eat,   Old clothes sent to the Island from the North for contraband's are sold to the white secesh sitizen's, by the sss^{tn} Superintendant Mr Sanderson,

   Genl these thing's are not gesse'd at but things that can be prove'd by those that saw them, and many more things that we can prove, Captn James. does not look after things, so Mr Sanderson has his own way   he now talk's of sending two hundred weman from Roanoke, then our family's will be sent one way and we in another direction,   most of the weman there are soldiers wives sent there by Genl Wild for protection,   must they be sent away when their husbands are in the army fighting.   we humbley ask you to look into these things, and do something for the negro's at Roanoke Island   we remain your humble servants

Ned Baxter

Saml Owen's

and forty three other contrabands from Roanoke Island *N.C.*[9]

HLSr

[*Endorsement*] Hd Qs 18th A[*rmy*]. C[*orps*].   Oct 6th 1864   I have the honor to state that quite a number or contrabands were employed at Roanoke Island to work on Fortifications, and that they have not been paid.   Gen. Weitzel has made repeated applications to the Chief Engr for funds to make these payments but he has not succeeded in obtaining them—   About four weeks ago Capt. Martin came to North Carolina to obtain laborers and, in order to obtain them in the shortest poss[ible] time it was thought best to take the gang which had been at work on fortifications.   As these men had not been paid and were very much in need of clothing &c. I took the responsibility of giving them certificates of ind[eb]tedness which enabled them to draw clothing and which will assist in identifying them when the funds come to pay them.   They were brought away by force but I think no one was authorized to tell them they were to be paid or practice any other deception complained of— Capt. Martin can doubtless give any other information in regard to the within petition—   Respectfully submitted   W. R. King 1st Lt US. Engrs

When faced with indifference or even hostility to their desire to reestablish their families, freedpeople—especially black soldiers— were not shy about asserting themselves. In many parts of the Union-occupied Confederacy, the families of black soldiers con- structed makeshift villages near the camps where their husbands, sons, and fathers served. The soldiers assisted them as they could, sharing food and clothing from their own military issues and

Former slaves selling produce, poultry, and hogs to Union officers, Beaufort, South Carolina.
(*Frank Leslie's Illustrated Newspaper,* Feb. 1, 1862)

"liberating" tools and other army equipment from their camps. The commander of a black regiment stationed near Memphis, seeing one such shantytown as a source of disorder and lawlessness, asked his superiors to clear the settlement and remove the soldiers' families to an island in the Mississippi River.

Memphis. Tenn.   Jan. 11th 1865

Sir.   There are several hundred negro women living in Temporary huts, between the camp of this regiment and the city, who have no visible means of support, and who are, for the most part, idle, lazy vagrants, committing depredations, and exercising a very pernicious influence over the colored soldiers of this Post.   They are generally in a destitute condition, and their wants are partially supplied by soldiers of colored regiments who claim them as wives.   The influence of these women over the members of my regiment is such, that I have great difficulty in keeping my men in camp nights, and have to be continually watchful and vigilent and enforc the severest penalties, in order to maintain any thing like satisfactory discipline, and attention to duties on the part of my men.   They also carry off rations from the companies in spite of the utmost vigilence of company commanders, and also carry off axes, shovels, spades, and picks, wherever they can be found, to use in building, and maintaining these households.   The soldiers of my regiment also steal each others clothing for their families to wear and dispose of.   I am compeled to enforce punishments continualy. for offences relating in some manner to these women.   Soldiers who are out nights are of no use while out of camp, and of very littl use for active duty when in camp.   The most serious obsticle I have to contend with in enforcing discipline arrises from this increasing evil.   As long as these women are allowed to remain where they are, it will be impossible to enforce that discipline which is requisite for efficiency, in my regiment; and I earnestly request for the benefit of the service, and for the sake of humanity, that these families be removed to Presidents Island where they will be much better cared for, and where they will be no detriment to the service, and society at large.   I am very respectfully Your Obdt. Servt.

HLS   John Foley[10]

> As a result of Colonel Foley's request, the superintendent of freed-men in the Memphis area received orders to move the soldiers' fam-ilies. He soon reported, however, that the freedpeople's resistance had thwarted his design.

Memphis, Tenn.,   24 Jany *1865.*

Captain: I have the honor to state, that in attempting to carry out the request made by Lieut Col Foley, in the inclosed communication, I detailed a guard of (12) Twelve men from Companies "B" and "K" 63[d] U.S.C.I. who with all the teams at my disposal, I sent with Lieut Bush to accomplish the work—   The Lieut commenced with a will, but has had very poor success on account of not having a stronger detail—   The people are unwilling to be moved, and will give no assistance themselves, but lock their doors, and run to their husbands in the various military organizations for protection—   The husbands swear their families shall not be moved to the Island and in some instances have come out under arms to prevent it

Owing to these and various other circumstances, all the men that I can send to the work are necessary for guards—

I would therefore request that a detail of (20) Twenty men with (4)

Four non-commissioned officers, be ordered to report at this office, for fatigue duty, daily—Sundays excepted—until the work of removal is accomplished.

The removal of this class of dependent and almost helpless people, together with the necessary provisions for their immediate comfort, is no light and withall a very unthankful job, and as my facilities are so circumscribed, I think that I may without presumption, ask the cooperation of all those who are alike interested— I am Capt Very Respectfully Your Obt. Servt.

T A Walker

I would also request a guard of ten men to accompany the detail called for   T A Walker   Capt & Supt Freedmen[11]

ALS

As the number of fugitive slaves grew, conditions in the contraband camps deteriorated. Poor sanitation, tainted water, and shortages of food, shelter, and medical care transformed these refuges into killing grounds, with federal superintendents becoming overseers of disaster rather than agents of relief. Such nightmarish conditions outraged the soldiers whose loved ones suffered and died at the hands of the very government they were defending. In Chattanooga, Tennessee, exasperated black soldiers who learned of conditions in a Nashville camp protested to their regimental commander, who appealed to departmental headquarters on their behalf.

Chattanooga, T[enn.], Jan 30 1865

Sir,   Many of the men of this Command have wives and families in some Camp (either "refugee" or "contraband") at Nashville,   The Stories that are brought me of the treatment these people receive, have determined me to address you this communication,— One man, just returned from furlough, informs me that the suffering from hungar & cold is so great that those wretched people are dying by scores—that sometimes thirty per day die & are carried out by wagon loads, without coffins, & thrown promiscuously, like brutes, into a trench—,

A few weeks ago the family,—wife & six small children—of an enlisted man of this regt, were sent from here to Nashville by order of the Post Comd'.— Today the children were brought back,—how or by whom I cannot learn, They are nearly starved, their limbs are frozen,—one of them is likely to loose both feet,— Their mother died in the camp at Nashville,— Why these children were not kept & taken care of instead of being sent back here I have no means of Knowing,

The men of my command appeal to me for relief from such treatment,— I cannot disregard their request,

I have therefore the honor most respy to lay this matter before the Comdg General & to most earnestly request that measures may be taken to relieve the condition of these most wretched people, Very respy Your obt servt

ALS   Jos. R. Putnam[12]

CHAPTER

SOLDIERS' FAMILIES IN THE FREE STATES

L IKE BLACK SOUTHERNERS, BLACK NORTHERNERS itched for an opportunity to strike a blow at slavery. Many had but recently escaped from bondage and were eager to meet slave-owners—their own or any reasonable facsimile—on the field of bat-tle. Others had friends and relatives still in captivity. Although free, black northerners were impoverished and despised, subject to rank discrimination, and denied the rights of white Americans. They understood their consignment to second-class citizenship as a product of the nation's commitment to slavery and believed eman-cipation would pave the way to equality. When the Emancipation Proclamation allowed black men to enlist in the Union army, those in the free states did so in numbers that were nothing less than astounding. By war's end, some 70 percent of northern black men of military age—nearly every able-bodied man—had served.

Enlistment was a family decision, since it entailed profound con-sequences for those who remained at home as well as for those who marched off to war. Proscribed from all but the most menial employment, black men and women earned their livelihoods on the fringes of the northern economy. Their material resources were shallow at best. To make ends meet, most households required the income of every resident adult. The absence and possible death of a breadwinner thus threatened not merely the stability of the northern black family but its very existence. For families whose savings were measured in coins and whose access to state and local relief was frequently obstructed by discriminatory policies and practices, unequal and irregular military pay posed a similar threat.

Distance compounded the problem, since northern soldiers served far from their homes. Whereas black men recruited in the South sometimes guarded the very contraband camps in which their wives, children, and parents had taken refuge, northern soldiers had to rely on furloughs, the press, and mail to maintain ties with dear ones at home. Their communications with family and with federal officials reflected, in various ways, how the war reshaped the lives of northern black soldiers and their kin.

If the enlistment of black men in the Union army elated black people and their white abolitionist allies, it shocked white southerners, who saw the arming of black men as an open invitation to slave insurrection. Confederate authorities refused to recognize black men in Union uniform as legitimate soldiers. Instead, they regarded them as slaves in insurrection and viewed their white officers as instigators of slave rebellion. At first, local Confederate commanders decided the fate of captured black soldiers and their officers, often executing them on the spot. In December 1862, however, Confederate President Jefferson Davis ordered the soldiers delivered to civil authorities in "the respective [Confederate] States to which they belong to be dealt with according to the laws of said States"; their officers were also to be remanded to state authorities.[1] Under state laws, the soldiers faced punishments ranging from enslavement to execution, and officers convicted of inciting insurrection were subject to execution or imprisonment.

Davis's proclamation infuriated and frightened the black community. For the parents, wives, and children of black men who had answered the Union's call, the threat was especially chilling. Hannah Johnson, whose son was serving in the 54th Massachusetts Infantry, wrote directly to Abraham Lincoln to express her outrage and to advise the president about his responsibilities as emancipator.

Buffalo [*N.Y.*]   July 31 1863

Excellent Sir   My good friend says I must write to you and she will send it   My son went in the 54th regiment.   I am a colored woman and my son was strong and able as any to fight for his country and the colored people have as much to fight for as any.   My father was a Slave and escaped from Louisiana before I was born morn forty years agone   I have but poor edication but I never went to schol, but I know just as well as any what is right between man and man.   Now I know it is right that a colored man should go and fight for his country, and so ought to a white man.   I know that a colored man ought to run no greater risques than a white, his pay is no greater his obligation to fight is the same. So why should not our enemies be compelled to treat him the same, Made to do it.

My son fought at Fort Wagoner but thank God he was not taken prisoner, as many were   I thought of this thing before I let my boy go but then they said M^r. Lincoln will never let them sell our colored soldiers for slaves,   if they do he will get them back quck   he will rettallyate and stop it.   Now Mr Lincoln dont you think you oght to stop this thing and make them do the same by the colored men   they have lived in idleness all their lives on stolen labor and made savages of the colored people, but they now are so furious because they are proving themselves to be men, such as have come away and got some edication.   It must not be so.   You must put the rebels to work in State prisons to making shoes and things, if they sell our colored soldiers, till they let them all go.   And give their wounded the same treatment.   it would seem cruel, but their no other way, and a just man must do hard things sometimes, that shew him to be a great man.   They tell me some do you will take back the Proclamation,   don't do it.   When you are dead and in Heaven, in a thousand years that action of yours will make the Angels sing your praises I know it.   Ought one man to own another, law for or not,   who made the law, surely the poor slave did not.   so it is wicked, and a horrible Outrage, there is no sense in it,   because a man has lived by robbing all his life and his father before him, should he complain because the stolen things found on him are taken.   Robbing the colored people of their labor is but a small part of the robbery   their souls are almost taken, they are made bruits of often.   You know all about this

Will you see that the colored men fighting now, are fairly treated. You ought to do this, and do it at once, Not let the thing run along   meet it quickly and manfully, and stop this, mean cowardly cruelty.   We poor oppressed ones, appeal to you, and ask fair play.   Yours for Christs sake

Hannah Johnson.

[*In another handwriting*] Hon. Mr. Lincoln   The above speaks for itself   Carrie Coburn[2]

ALS

> Unbeknown to Hannah Johnson, Lincoln had only the previous day promised to retaliate if captured black soldiers were denied the rights of prisoners of war. Although Confederates both executed and enslaved captured black soldiers, Lincoln did not make good on his threat.

COLORED SOLDIERS!

EQUAL STATE RIGHTS!

AND MONTHLY PAY WITH WHITE MEN!!

On the 1st day of January, 1863, the President of the United States proclaimed

FREEDOM TO OVER

THREE MILLIONS OF SLAVES!

This decree is to be enforced by all the power of the Nation.   On the 21st of July last he issued the following order:—

PROTECTION OF COLORED TROOPS.

" WAR DEPARTMENT, ADJUTANT GENERAL'S OFFICE,)
Washington, July 21.   )

" *General Order, No. 233.*

"The following order of the President is published for the information and government of all concerned:—

EXECUTIVE MANSION, Washington, July 30.

'" It is the duty of every Government to give protection to its citizens, of whatever class, color, or condition, and especially to those who are duly organized as soldiers in the public service.   The law of nations, and the usages and customs of war, as carried on by civilized powers, permit no distinction as to color in the treatment of prisoners of war as public enemies.   To sell or enslave any captured person on account of his color, is a relapse into barbarism, and a crime against the civilization of the age.

'" The Government of the United States will give the same protection to all its soldiers, and if the enemy shall sell or enslave any one because of his color, the offence shall be punished by retaliation upon the enemy's prisoners in our possession.   It is, therefore, ordered, for every soldier of the United States, killed in violation of the laws of war, a rebel soldier shall be executed; and for every one enslaved by the enemy, or sold into slavery, a rebel soldier shall be placed at hard labor on the public works, and continued at such labor until the other shall be released and receive the treatment due to prisoners of war.

'" ABRAHAM LINCOLN." '

'" By order of the Secretary of War.

'" E. D. TOWNSEND, Assistant Adjutant General." '

That the President is in earnest the rebels soon began to find out, as witness the following order from his Secretary of War:—

" WAR DEPARTMENT, Washington City, August 8, 1863.

" SIR:—Your letter of the 3d inst., calling the attention of this Department to the cases of Orin H. Brown, William H. Johnston, and Wm. Wilson, three colored men captured on the gunboat Isaac Smith, has received consideration.   This Department has directed that three rebel prisoners of South Carolina, if there be any such in our possession, and if not, three others, be confined in close custody and held as hostages for Brown, Johnston, and Wilson, and that the fact be communicated to the rebel authorities at Richmond.

" Very respectfully your obedient servant,

" EDWIN M. STANTON, Secretary of War.

" The Hon. GIDEON WELLES, Secretary of the Navy."

And retaliation will be our practice now—man for man—to the bitter end.

Recruitment broadside promising equal pay to black soldiers. (National Archives)

Among the assurances black families received when their husbands, sons, and fathers enlisted in the Union army was that black
and white soldiers would earn the same pay. They did not. Whereas
white privates received $13 a month, plus a $3 clothing allowance,
black soldiers received $10 a month, from which $3 was deducted
for clothing. To add to the affront, black noncommissioned officers
received the same pay as black privates. The failure of the federal
government to live up its promise, the insult implicit in unequal
pay, and the lower pay itself elicited a hail of protests from black
soldiers and their kin. When Hiram A. Peterson, a sergeant from
New York, informed his father about the government's policy, his
father sought an explanation from the secretary of war.

Scio   Allegany County   State of New York   Oct. 29th 1863.
Dr Sir   I have a son now in the service of the U.S. who was drafted
from this town in the month of July last. (he is colored.) and after being
taken from this place to rendezvous at Elmira was sent to Washington
and is now First Duty Sargeant. (at Camp Casey) in Co. G. 2nd. U.S.
colored troops.   he has recd one month pay at $7.   now what I wish to
know, is whether the sum of Seven dollars, per month is all that colored
drafted men from this state are entitled to.   my son supposed & so did I
that he would receive the same pay, as white Soldiers   he is a truly
loyal Boy and says, he will serve his Country faithfully. but thinks there
must be something wrong in relation to his receiving only Seven dollars
per month. pay.   I inclosed a letter, he wrote home, making inquiry as to
the matter.   your reply will settle the matter and will be appreciated, by,
a colored man who, is willing to sacrafice his son in the cause of Freedom
& Humanity   Yours Very Respectfully

ALS   Aaron Peterson[3]

[*Enclosure*]   Camp Casey [*D.C.*]   Oct 24 [*1863*]
sir   i take this Liberty to wright to you to let you no how soldiering

goes with   it all goes very well and i am content with every thing but my pay and i never can bee, contented untill i get my rits   i am first duty sargt and my pay should bee 17 dolars a month and i think it is hard to bee abliged to poot up with sevan dolars   i thought you might giv me some infamation about it if you will pleas rite to me   i am willing to bee a soldier and serve my time faithful like a man but i think it is hard to bee poot off in sutch a dogesh maner as that

it haint enough to pay postage on my letters so i shall hav to send this with out a stamp for i haint money enough to buy a stamp

remember me to the boys   Yours

Hiram A Peterson

7 dolars a month and half rations is rather hard

Excuse my boldnes but pleas answer this and obelege   yours Sargt H A Peterson[4]

ALS

While some black soldiers and their families lamented unequal wages, others complained about the army's failure to pay them at all. Tardy and irregular payments weighed heavily on wives and children at home, for most black women were limited to employment as domestics and washerwomen, at wages only a fraction of those earned by men. To make matters worse, some northern states and localities denied them access to special funds created for the relief of the families of Union soldiers. The wife of a New Jersey soldier wrote directly to President Lincoln about her predicament.

Mt Holly [*N.J.*]   July 11 1864

Sir,   my husband, who is in Co. K. 22nd Reg't U.S. Col[d] Troops. (and now in the Macon Hospital at Portsmouth with a wound in his arm) has not received any pay since last May and then only thirteen dollars.   I write to you because I have been told you would see to it. I have four children to support and I find this a great strugle. A hard life this!

I being a col^d woman do not get any State pay. Yet my husband is fighting for the country. Very Resp'y yours

Rosanna Henson[5]

ALS

Refusing as a matter of principle to accept unequal pay—even when their state legislature offered to make up the difference between the amount promised and the federal government's actual remission—some black regiments took a stand against discrimination within the army of liberation. In a remonstrance to the president, members of the 55th Massachusetts Infantry explained why they had left their homes and families to fight a distant enemy and intimated forceful action if their grievances went unaddressed.

Folly island   South Carolina   July 16th 18.64

Sir   We The Members of Co D of the 55th Massechusetts vols Call the attention of your Excellency to our case

1st   First We wase enlisted under the act of Congress of July 18.61 Placing the officers non Commissioned officers & Privates of the volunteer forces in all Respects as to Pay on the footing of Similar Corps of the Regular Army   2nd   We Have Been in the Field now thirteen months & a Great many yet longer   We Have Recieved no Pay & Have Been offered only seven Dollars Pr month Which the Paymaster Has said was all He Had ever Been authorized to Pay Colored Troops   this was not acording to our enlistment   Consequently We Refused the Money   the Commonwealth of Massechusetts then Passed an act to make up all Deficienceys which the general Government Refused To Pay But this We Could not Recieve as The Troops in the general service are not Paid Partly By Government & Partly By State   3rd   that to us money is no object   we came to fight For Liberty justice & Equality. These are gifts we Prise more Highly than Gold   For these We Left our Homes our Familys Friends & Relatives most Dear to take as it ware our Lives in our Hands To Do Battle for God & Liberty

4th   after the elaps of over thirteen months spent cheerfully & willingly Doing our Duty most faithfuly in the Trenches Fatiegue Duty in camp and conspicious valor & endurence in Battle as our Past History will Show

P 5th   therefore we Deem these sufficient Reasons for Demanding our Pay from the Date of our inlistment & our imediate Discharge Having Been enlisted under False Prentence as the Past History of the Company will Prove

6th   Be it further Resolved that if imediate steps are not takened to Relieve us we will Resort to more stringent mesures

We have the Honor to Remin your Obedint Servants   The members of Co D

HLS   [*74 signatures*]6

Although word had not yet reached the regiments stationed in South Carolina, Congress had equalized the pay of black and white soldiers on June 15, 1864, retroactive to the first of the year. The legislation further provided that those black soldiers who had been free at the beginning of the war were entitled to receive the pay allowed by law at the time of their enlistment—which, the attorney general ruled, meant that they were owed the same pay as white soldiers from the date of their enlistment.7

The families of protesting black soldiers paid a high price for their principles. While the men continued to receive rations and uniforms even when they refused to accept unequal pay, their wives and children received nothing and were left to support themselves without the assistance of their husbands, sons, and fathers. Rachel Ann Wicker, the wife of an Ohio soldier who had enlisted in the 55th Massachusetts, added her voice to the chorus of protests from the soldiers themselves. Her reference to the effects of wartime inflation identified a subject of great concern to the families of black soldiers, for while prices soared during the war, the wages of domestic servants and washerwomen changed hardly at all. Writing to "Mr. President Andrew" (either the governor of Massachusetts or the president of the United States), Wicker spoke for herself as well as other black women who, with their men off to war, bore the full weight of family responsibilities.

Piqua   Miama Co   ohio   Sep 12 1864

Sir   i write to you to know the reason why our husbands and sons who enlisted in the 55 Massichusette regiment have not Bin paid off   i speak for my self and Mother and i know of a great many others as well as ourselve are suffering for the want of money to live on   when provision and Clotheing wer Cheap we might have got a long   But Every thing now is thribbl and over what it was some thre year Back   But it matters not if Every thing was at the old Price   i think it a Piece of injustice to have those soldiers there 15 months with out a cent of Money   for my part i Cannot see why they have not th same rite to their 16 dollars per month as th Whites or Even th Coulord Soldiers that went from ohio   i think if Massichusette had left off Comeing to other States for Soldiers th Soldirs would have bin Better off and Massichusette saved her Credit   i wish you if you pleas to Answer this Letter and tell me Why it is that you Still insist upon them takeing 7 dollars a month when you give the Poorest White Regiment that has went out 16 dollars   Answer this if you Pleas and oblige Your humble Servant

ALS   Rachel Ann Wicker[8]

Writing as one of the "Grandsons of Mother Africa," Thomas Sipple, a soldier from New York, employed that familial metaphor in
describing how the federal government's failure to pay him had
worked a hardship on his family. His letter to President Lincoln—
affirmed by comrades from Delaware and New York—reveals that,
even if he succeeded in obtaining wages equal to those of white soldiers, his kin were paying dearly for their patriotism. While they
were ready to sacrifice in order to put down the rebellion, Sipple
was unwilling to see them suffer as a result of bureaucratic ineffi-
ciency and indifference.

New Orleans   Louisiana   Camp Parpit   [*August*] 1864
My Dear and Worthy Friend MR. President.   I thake this oppertunity of
interducing my self to you By wrteing thes fiew Lines To let you know
that you have Proven A friend to me and to all our Race   And now i
stand in the Defence of the Country myself Ready and Willing to oBay
all orders & demands that has A tendency to put Down this Rebelion In
military Life or Civel Life.   I Enlisted at Almira state of N. York,
shemoung County Under *Mr* C. W. Cawing Provose Marshall And
[*when*] I Enlisted he told me i would get 13 Dollars Per. Mounth or more
if White Soldiers got it   he expected the wages would Raise And i
would get my pay every 2 Months   hear i am in the survice 7 months
And have Not Recived Eney Monthly Pay   I have a wife and 3 Children
Neither one of them Able to thake Care of Themselfs and my wife is sick
And she has sent to me for money   And i have No way of geting Eney
money to send to her Because i cant Get my Pay.   And it gos very hard
with me to think my family should be At home A suffering have money
earnt and cant not get it   And I Dont know when i will Be Able to
Releave my suffering Family   And another thing when I Enlisted I was
promised A furlow and I have Not had it   Please MR Lincom Dont
think I Am Blameing you for it   I Dident think you knew Eney thing

About it   And I Dident know eney Other Course to thake To obtain
what I think is Right   I invested my money in Percuring A house an
home for my wife and Children   And she write to me she has to work
and can not surport the Children with out my Aid   When I was At
home i could earn from 26 to 28 Dollars A Month   When I Enlisted it
told i was to have the same Bounty Clothing and Ration as the Soldier
and 325 Dollars wich the 25 Dollars i Never got   I Dont Beleave the
Goverment wants me eney how   In fact i mean the New York 20th
Regiment   The Reason why i say so is Because we are treated Like A
Parcels of Rebs   I Do not say the Goverment is useing us so   I [*do
not*] Believe the Government knows Eney thing About how we are
treated   we came out to be true union soldiers the Grandsons of
Mother Africa Never to Flinch from Duty   Please Not to thinks I Am
finding fault with the rules of the Goverment   If this Be the rules i am
willing to Abide by them   I wonce Before was a Slave 25 years   I
made escape 1855 Came In to York state from Maryland   And i
Enlisted in the survice got up By the union Legue Club   And we ware
Promised All satisfaction Needful   But it seem to Be A failure   We
Are not treated Like we are soldiers in coleague Atall   we are Deprived
of the most importances things we Need in health and sickness Both
That surficint Food And quality   As for The sick it is A shocking thing
to Look into thire conditions   Death must Be thire Doom when once
they have to go to the Hospital   Never Return Again   such is the
medical Assistance of the 20th Rig n.y   your sarvent under Arms
sincerely

> George Rodgers
>
> Thomas Sipple   Wilmington Delaware.
>
> Samuel Sampson

[*In another handwriting*] Mr President   I Surtify that this I is jest

what mr Rodgers sais and my other frend mr Sipele   Nimrod
Rowley   Elmira Chemong CO. N.Y.

[*In the original handwriting*] Pease excuse your Needy Petishners   We
most heartly wish you the intire victory over All Your Enemys.   And A
spedy sucsess To the Commander-in Chief of the Army And Navy   And
may Peace Forever Reighn[9]

HLS

> Without support from their fathers, sons, and husbands, soldiers'
> families turned to the public for support. Many northern states and
> localities established funds for just such purposes, since even at full
> pay, remitted in timely fashion, it was often difficult for soldiers'
> families—white or black—to make ends meet. But relief funds
> grew thin as the war dragged on and disappeared almost entirely
> once victory had been achieved. In some places, the families of
> black soldiers were excluded from such assistance altogether, and,
> where they were not, they were generally the first to be terminated
> when the money ran short. A soldier's wife who found herself desti-
> tute when she was cut off asked the secretary of war either to send
> her husband home to ensure his family a livelihood or to assist her
> in joining him.

Detroit Michigan   May 27 instant 1865

Sir   I take the privelige of writing to you asking A favour of you if it is
in your power to grant that is to give my Husband John Wesley Wilson
A furloah   My Husband belonges to the 102d U.S. Colored regiment
and is the leader of the regimental Band now Station at Beaufort
S.C.   or will you please to give me Transportation to Beaufort S.C.   if
had money I would not ask you for a Pass   John Wesley Wilson has not
recevied any pay from the government for nine mounths and it leaves me

Insignia from flag of the 3rd U.S. Colored Infantry.
(Freedmen and Southern Society Project)

compleatly distitute   I have no support except what I earn by my own labor from day to day   the relief fund that I have been receiving has been cut of[f] through prejudices to Color and it leaves me compleatly distitute of means for my support   Michigan has no respect for her Colored Soldiers or their famileys.   My Husband has been in the army one year and half and i am very anxous to see him and by giving me Transportation to Beaufort S.C. you would Confer a great favour on your well wisher   Your Obedient Servent

ALS   Mrs John W. Wilson[10]

> The destitution Mrs. Wilson experienced was shared by many other black families. The difficulty of obtaining relief was compounded when a soldier from one place was credited against the enlistment quota of another, and, as a result, local officials denied his family any support. Such circumstances drove many a soldier to desperation, as news of his family's suffering reached him in some distant quarter and he had no way to provide for them. George Freeman, a member of the same Michigan regiment as Mrs. Wilson's husband, vented his frustration to the chief justice of the United States. With the war at an end, Private Freeman saw no reason for him to be kept from returning home to fulfill his familial responsibilities.

General Hospitle   Beaufort SC   June 25th *1865.*

Dear, Sir,   I am under the painfull necesity of writing you a few lines for Redresse   I hav been in The Sirvice of the united states since Nov fifth one thousand eight hundred and sixty four and hav never recieve pay but twice once in June sixty four and then in, August   What you paid me in June was seven doll. Per months   I hav not recieved my Back pay From the goverment yet   I am a man of faimley a Wife and two small children   I was fooled in the first place   my famley Recieves no

Relief from my state as was Promesed me For I was stolen from my
town of Enrollment and creadet to the city of Detroit, state of Michigan
by H. Barnes the one that got up the Regtment for the state of
Michigan   I could tell you Of a great deal of rascality that has Ben a
going on in the Regtment that I belong if it was nesicary but I only want
obliging my self   as you are one of the head of our great Governent I
write you for assistance   I want them to Give me my discharge and let
me go and worke and suporte my Familey for they are nearly starved
and hav not suitabal cloathing to hide thair neckedness   my famley
depends upon my daily labor for their suporte   when I enterd the
service i felt it my Duty to go   I weryed along all to my duty untill
about the last two months   I hav ben in the Hospitle   I went with out
Pay nearly all of the time I hav ben out   now the ware is over I think
that it is no moore than wright that I should Have my Discharge as I
was sick and in the hospitle before the order was Ishued to discharge
men in hospitle   Some of the officers has eaven taken the mens
Discharge papers away from them in the 32nd USC Troops   Is that
right   some officers will not send the mens discriptive list to
them   that is the case with me   If I hav don wrong in writing to my
superior i pray Pardon me For so doing But I should like to Recieve
some money from the Governent and go and see after my fanliey

Nomore From your moste humble Servent and Solgier

George G Freeman

I am a colord man one that has no advantage[11]

ALS

CHAPTER

IV.

SOLDIERS' FAMILIES IN
THE BORDER STATES

IKE THEIR COUNTERPARTS IN THE FREE STATES,
border-state soldiers and their kin experienced lengthy separation, unreliable means of communication, and economic distress.
Unlike their northern counterparts, however, soldiers' families in
the border states also grappled with burdens imposed by slavery.

The Emancipation Proclamation had no bearing on the slave
states that had remained in the Union—Delaware, Maryland,
Kentucky, and Missouri. Slavery retained full standing within their
bounds. Although military activity at times created opportunities
for slaves to escape their bondage, official policy dictated support
for the slaveholders' authority.

With slavery still legal and the Emancipation Proclamation
inapplicable, enlistment in the Union army offered the sole route to
freedom. Politically powerful border-state slaveowners forestalled
recruitment until months after black men began entering the ranks
in the free states and in the Union-occupied Confederacy. When
recruitment offices eventually opened, slaveholders obstructed
their slaves' efforts to enlist. But the slaves were not deterred.

Seeing enlistment as an opportunity to gain their own freedom and to fight for the liberation of their families, border-state black men joined the Union army in great numbers and in proportions exceeding those of the other slave states.

Large-scale enlistment dealt a fatal blow to slavery in the border states. But the process it set in motion was a slow and painful one, in the course of which the soldiers' families often paid a high price. Slaveholders threatened to punish the families of men who enlisted—and then made good their threats. They forced the wives and children of black soldiers to do heavy work normally reserved for able-bodied men. Or, viewing the women and children as unwanted burdens, they turned them out to fend for themselves.

The abuse of their families infuriated black soldiers. But their protests fell on deaf ears, because federal military officials insisted that the families were legally still slaves and the army therefore lacked authority to intervene. Nor did the army establish contraband camps to house and protect soldiers' families, as it did in Union-occupied parts of the Confederacy. Instead, federal authorities refused to assume any responsibility for fugitive slaves in the border states on the grounds that slavery was still in force and the owners were responsible for their maintenance.

The wives, children, and other kin of most border-state black soldiers thus remained under the control of their owners, still held as slaves. Those who escaped to federal encampments had no guarantee of food, shelter, or protection. Many who gained admission were later expelled. As their husbands, sons, and fathers fought under the banner of freedom, black soldiers' families in the border states endured the death throes of slavery at first hand.

———•———

In Missouri, it was not until November 1863 that black recruitment began in earnest. But once federal authorities announced they would accept any able-bodied man of African descent, regardless of his owner's loyalty or consent, the floodgates opened. Slaves who risked escape and made their way to the recruiters' headquarters had to leave their families behind, however, for federal officials accepted none but men of military age. As a result, black soldiers'

wives, children, and parents remained in the custody of slaveowners who were embittered by the men's enlistment. Martha Glover
described to her husband the burdens she had borne since he joined
the army.

Mexico Mo   Dec 30th 1863

My Dear Husband   I have received your last kind letter a few days ago
and was much pleased to hear from you once more.   It seems like a long
time since you left me.   I have had nothing but trouble since you
left.   You recollect what I told you how they would do after you was
gone.   they abuse me because you went & say they will not take care of
our children & do nothing but quarrel with me all the time and beat me
scandalously the day before yesterday—   Oh I never thought you would
give me so much trouble as I have got to bear now.   You ought not to left
me in the fix I am in & all these little helpless children to take care of.   I
was invited to a party to night but I could not go   I am in too much
trouble to want to go to parties.   the children talk about you all the
time.   I wish you could get a furlough & come to see us once more.   We
want to see you worse than we ever did before.   Remember all I told you
about how they would do me after you left—for they do worse than they
ever did & I do not know what will become of me & my poor little children.   Oh I wish you had staid with me & not gone till I could go with
you for I do nothing but grieve all the time about you.   write & tell me
when you are coming.

Tell Isaac that his mother come & got his clothes   she was so sorry
he went.   You need not tell me to beg any more married men to go.   I
see too much trouble to try to get any more into trouble too—   Write to
me & do not forget me & my children—   farewell my dear husband from
your wife

ALS   Martha[1]

Slaveowners made it difficult for black soldiers to communicate with their wives and children, let alone attend to their needs— needs that became increasingly desperate as vindictive masters and mistresses stinted on provisions and clothing. In a letter penned for her by a sympathetic neighbor, the wife of a Missouri soldier warned her husband against sending letters or money in care of her owner, for fear he would intercept them.

Paris Mo   Jany 19, 1864

My Dear Husband   I r'ecd your letter dated Jan'y 9th also one dated Jany 1st but have got no one till now to write for me.   You do not know how bad I am treated.   They are treating me worse and worse every day. Our child cries for you.   Send me some money as soon as you can for me and my child are almost naked.   My cloth is yet in the loom and there is no telling when it will be out.   Do not send any of your letters to Hogsett especially those having money in them as Hogsett will keep the money.   George Combs went to Hannibal soon after you did so I did not get that money from him.   Do the best you can and do not fret too much for me for it wont be long before I will be free and then all we make will be ours.   Your affectionate wife

Ann

P.S.   Sind our little girl a string of beads in your next letter to remember you by.   Ann[2]

HLSr

[*Endorsement*] Andy if you send me any more letters for your wife do not send them in the care of any one.   Just direct them plainly to James A Carney Paris Monroe County Mo.   Do not write too often   Once a month will be plenty and when you write do not write as though you had recd any letters for if you do your wife will not be so apt to get them.

Hogsett has forbid her coming to my house so we cannot read them to
her privately.   If you send any money I will give that to her myself.   Yrs
&c   Jas A Carney

> The vulnerability of their families to reprisals by slaveholders dis-
> heartened black soldiers. Morale plummeted when they learned of
> the mistreatment of those they had left behind. Seeing the effect on
> military discipline, some company officers urged their superiors to
> take action. Lieutenant William P. Deming relayed to the general
> in charge of black recruitment in Missouri two reports that slave-
> owners were punishing soldiers' wives and children by assigning
> them heavy work normally done by the men.

Benton Barracks   Mo   Feb 1st 1864
Sir,   Complaint has been made to me, by Martin Patterson, of Co. "H,"
2d Missouri Vols of A[*frican*]. D[*escent*]. that he has direct and reliable
information from home that his family is receiving ill treatment from
James Patterson their master, of Fayette, Howard Co. Mo

He says, that his wife is compelled to do out door work,—such as chop
wood, husk corn &c. and that one of his children has been suffered to
freeze, and has sinc died

Further complaint has been made by Wm Brooks that his wife and
children are receiving ill treatment from Jack Sutter their master, of
Fayette, Howard Co. Mo.   He says that they are required to do the
same work that he formerly had to do, such as chopping wood, splitting
rails &c

The said Martin Patterson and Wm Brooks request that permission be
granted to remove their families to Jefferson City   Yours Respectfuly
ALS   William P Deming[3]

Having lost the labor of the men, slaveholders increasingly saw enlistees' wives and children as unwanted dependents. Some were evicted by force. Reporting one such incident and knowing that others would follow, a Union officer sought instructions from headquarters.

Fulton M° March 28th 1864

Colonel. The wife of a colored recruit came into my Office to night and says she has been severely beaten and driven from home by her master and owner. She has a child some two years old with her, and says she left two larger ones at home, She desires to be sent forward with her husband; says she is willing to work and expects to do so at home or elsewhere; that her master told her never to return to him; that his men were all gone, and that he could not, and would not support the women. What is proper for me to do in such cases? I know many such will occur. Several persons have asked me the question. "What are we to do with the women and children"? the men are in the army; we cannot raise enough for them to eat. I am well convinced that threats are made, that in case the men go away, the women will be turned out of door. The owner of the woman refered to, is an aged man, a most inveterate rebel, and has, or did have when the war commenced, four sons in the rebel army. I am Colonel Very Respectfully Your Obedient Servant

ALS   Hiram Cornell[4]

The colonel addressed by Cornell characterized his request as "one of dozen's of similar applications of like character."[5]

———•———

With almost 40 percent of the state's black men of military age serving in the Union army, with slaveholders eager to rid themselves of dependent slaves, and with Confederate sympathizers either exiled or disfranchised, Missouri voters in the fall of 1864 elected delegates to a constitutional convention that would consider measures to abolish slavery. While the convention deliberated, a Union officer reported, some slaveholders executed a preemptive emancipation of their own.

Hannibal Mo   Jan. 12th 1865—

Sir— I find that many of the Citizens of my Sub: Dist: especially the disloyal element—are anticipating the action of the state convention and send their negroes adrift at such time as it suits them—and it is working very badly indeed up here—   The negro men have left their masters some time since—and those now on hand are principally women & children—and they being found rather unprofitable, and expensive—are turned loose upon the people to support—   Their former owners make no provision for them, save hauling them to within a convenient distance of some military post, and set them out with orders to never return home—telling them they are free.   There has one case come to my knowledge where the sons of an old man—drove the negroes off from the place—because the old man began to show signs of recognizing five of his servants as half brothers & sisters to his children lawfully begotten—   I have in two instances ordered that the former owners shall take care of these helpless negroes until some other provision is made for them—and I think some action should be taken to let the rebels generally know that they shall not shirk in this manner.   They, I think, fear the convention will resolve—that they shall take care of their helpless negroes on hand, until they get large enough to take care of themselves—

. . . .

John F. Tyler—⁶

ALS

In Kentucky, politically powerful slaveholders managed to delay the recruitment of black soldiers until the spring of 1864. Once underway, however, recruitment drew enormous numbers into military ranks; by the end of the war, nearly 60 percent of the eligible black men had enlisted, the largest proportion of any slave state. As in Missouri, the families of black soldiers generally remained under their owners' control, and slaveholders showed little restraint in dealing with those still subject to their authority. Indeed, viewing black recruitment as both a threat to the slave system and a deeply personal insult, slaveholders vented their anger and frustration on the soldiers' families. Patsey Leach, whose husband was killed in battle only weeks after enlisting, described her ordeal.

　　　　　　　　　　　　　　　Camp Nelson Ky　25" March 1865

Personally appeared before me J　M Kelley Notary Public in and for the County of Jessamine State of Kentucky Patsey Leach a woman of color who being duly sworn according to law doth depose and say—

I am a widow and belonged to Warren Wiley of Woodford County Ky. My husband Julius Leach was a member of Co. D. 5" U.S. C[*olored*]. Cavalry and was killed at the Salt Works Va. about six months ago. When he enlisted sometime in the fall of 1864 he belonged to Sarah Martin Scott County Ky.　He had only been about a month in the service when he was killed.　I was living with aforesaid Wiley when he died.　He knew of my husbands enlisting before I did but never said any thing to me about it.　From that time he treated me more cruelly than ever whipping me frequently without any cause and insulting me on every occasion.　About three weeks after my husband enlisted a Company of Colored Soldiers passed our house and I was there in the garden and looked at them as they passed.　My master had been watching me and when the soldiers had gone I went into the kitchen. My master followed me and Knocked me to the floor senseless saying as he did so, "You have been looking at them darned Nigger

Soldiers"   When I recovered my senses he beat me with a cowhide
When my husband was Killed my master whipped me severely saying my
husband had gone into the army to fight against white folks and he my
master would let me know that I was foolish to let my husband go he
would "take it out of my back," he would "Kill me by picemeal" and he
hoped "that the last one of the nigger soldiers would be Killed"   He
whipped me twice after that using similar expressions   The last
whipping he gave me he took me into the Kitchen tied my hands tore all
my clothes off until I was entirely naked, bent me down, placed my head
between his Knees, then whipped me most unmercifully until my back
was lacerated all over, the blood oozing out in several places so that I
could not wear my underclothes without their becoming saturated with
blood.   The marks are still visible on my back.   On this and other
occasions my master whipped me for no other cause than my husband
having enlisted.   When he had whipped me he said "never mind God
dam you when I am done with you tomorrow you never will live no
more."   I knew he would carry out his threats so that night about 10
o'clock I took my babe and travelled to Arnolds Depot where I took the
Cars to Lexington   I have five children,   I left them all with my
master except the youngest and I want to get them but I dare not go
near my master knowing he would whip me again.   My master is a
Rebel Sympathizer and often sends Boxes of Goods to Rebel prisoners.
And further Deponent saith not.

Her
Signed   Patsey   Leach[7]
mark

HDcSr

Sure that they would become targets of abuse if they remained in
their owners' custody, black families sought admission into military camps and posts. But in the border states, where slavery

remained legal, federal authorities generally refused food and protection to fugitive slaves, on the grounds that their owners were legally responsible for their support. Still, sympathetic officers could sometimes be found. John Burnside took his family with him into Camp Nelson, near Lexington, Kentucky, after receiving explicit assurances from one such officer. Hundreds of other former slaves gathered there as well, most of them the relatives of men who, like Burnside, had joined the Union army. Then, in November 1864, after months of futile efforts to forbid entry to new refugees and remove those already there, the commander at Camp Nelson expelled the women, children, and old people. In an affidavit sworn before military authorities, John Burnside described the expulsion of his wife and ailing daughter.

Camp Nelson Ky.　Dec. [15,] 1864.

Personally appeared before me. E. B W. Restieaux Capt and A[ssistant]. Q[uarter]. M[aster]. John Burnside—a man of color who being sworn upon oath says— I am a soldier in Company K. 124 Regt. U. S.C.T. I am a married man. My wife and children belonged to William Royster of Garrard County Ky. Royster had a son John who was with [Confederate General John H.] Morgan during his raid into Kentucky in June 1863. He got separated from Morgan's command and went home. The Provost Marshal instituted a search for him at two different times He was not found. My family were charged with giving the information which led to the measures of the Provost Marshal. William Royster told me that my wife had been trying to ruin him for the last two years and if he found that this—meaning the information went out through the black family—meaning my family— he would scatter them to the four winds of heaven. This was said about the last of September 1864. In consequence of this threat my family were in constant dread, and desired to find protection and employment from the Government. At that time I had been employed at Camp

Nelson and was not enlisted.   A few days afterward I was sick at my
mothers.   I sent my sister to see Col. Sedgwick[*] and inquire if my
family might come to Camp, and if they might, would they be protected:
She returned the same night and informed me that Col. Sedgwick said
tell him (me) to bring them in and I, Col Sedgwick, will protect them.
Before, I was unwilling that they should come but on receiving the
promised protection of Col. Sedgwick. I told them to come.   While my
wife and family were in Camp they never received any money or
provision from the government but earned their living with hard work

On Friday afternoon Nov. 28. [*25*] 1864 the Provost guard ordered
my wife and family out of Camp.   The guard had a wagon into which
my wife and family were forced to go and were then driven out the lines

They were driven to a wood belonging to Mr. Simpson about seven
miles from Camp and there thrown out without any protection or any
home.   While they were in the wood it rained hard and my family were
exposed to the storm.   My eldest daughter had been sick for some time
and was then slowly recovering.   and further this deponent saith not.

HDcSr   John Burnside[8]

> A northern missionary, challenging the idea that the families at
> Camp Nelson had been a charge on government resources,
> denounced the callousness with which they had been expelled.

                                        Camp Nelson Ky   Dec. 16" 1864

Personally appeared before me E B W Restieaux Capt and
A[*ssistant*]. Q[*uarter*]. M[*aster*]. Abisha Scofield who being duly sworn
upon oath says.   I am a clergyman of the congregational denomination

---

[*]Thomas D. Sedgwick was in charge of the organization of black troops
at Camp Nelson.

and have been laboring among the Freedmen at Camp Nelson Ky. under the auspices of the American Missionary association since the 20th of Sept 1864.   The families of the colored solders who were in Camp lived in cabins and huts erected by the colored solders or at the expense of the women.   During my labors among them I have witnessed about fifty of these huts and cabins erected and the material of which they were constructed was unserviceable to the Government.   I have had extensive dealing with these people and from my observation I believe that they supported themselves by washing cooking and &c.

Until the 22nd of last November I never heard any objection made by the military authorities of the Post to the women and children of colored soldiers residing within the limits of the camp.   On Tuesday the 22nd of November last the huts and cabins in which the families of the colored soldiers lived were torn down and the inhabitants were placed in Government wagons and driven outside the lines.   The weather at the time was the coldest of the season.   The wind was blowing quite sharp and the women and children were thinly clad and mostly without shoes. They were not all driven out on one day but their expulsion occupied about three days.

When they were driven out I did not know where they were to be taken and on the following Sabbath Nov 27" I went in search of the exiles.   I found them in Nicholasville about six miles from Camp scattered in various places.   Some were in an old Store house, some were straying along and lying down in the highway and all appeared to be suffering from exposure to the weather.   I gave them some food.   I received the provisions from Capt T. E. Hall A[*ssistant*]. Q[*uarter*]. M[*aster*].

The food was absolutely needed.   On Monday Nov. 28 I saw and conversed with about sixteen women and children who had walked from Nicholasville in the hopes of getting into Camp.   The guard refused them admittance.   I told the guard that the order by which the women and children were expelled had been countermanded.   The guard told me that he had strict orders not to admit them   They were not admitted.   Among the number was a young woman who was quite sick and while I was conversing with the guard she lay on the ground.   A day or two after this they were allowed to return to Camp.   They were then very destitute most all complaining of being unwell.   Children trembling with cold and wearied with fatigue.   Since that time they have been crowded in a school room in Camp and their condition has been most abject and miserable, whereas they were pretty comfortable before they were driven out.   While out of Camp they incurred disease and are now suffering from the effects of this exposure   As a clergyman I have no hesitation in pronouncing the treatment to which these poor people have been subjected as exceedingly demoralizing in its effects in addition to the physical suffering it entailed.   And further this deponent saith not

HDeSr   (Signed)   Abisha Scofield[9]

> The vocal opposition of missionaries and sympathetic officers, which received wide publicity in northern newspapers, forced the government to readmit the banished women and children into Camp Nelson, although not before the expulsions had caused suffering and at least one death.*

> Black soldiers' concern for their families mounted when the army removed the men to distant battlefronts. The commander of a Kentucky regiment described to his brigade commander how the continued enslavement of the soldiers' families made it nearly impossible for the men to communicate with them, much less provide material support.

*See pp. 199–201.

Families of former slaves arriving at Baltimore. (*Frank Leslie's Illustrated Newspaper*, Sept. 30, 1869)

In the Field—Va.   February 6th 1865.

Sir:

. . . .

In behalf of the enlisted men of the Regiment and their families, it is my duty to inform you of the peculiar circumstances under which they are placed, with the hope that it will sooner or later be brought to the notice of the Government, and such action be taken as will remedy the evil.

All the men of the Regiment were recruited in Kentucky.   A large proportion of them were slaves previous to entering the service.   A large number of them have families still remaining in servitude, who are most shamefully and inhumanly treated by their masters in consequence of their husbands having enlisted in the union army.   It is the highest ambition of a large number to mitigate and relieve their wants by remittances whereby some of the necessary wants and comforts of life may be given them.

A moment's reflection will prove to any one that it is impossible under the existing circumstances to alleviate their wants in the slightest degree.   Unable to read or write they are entirely dependent upon their masters for any information they may receive from husbands and friends who are in the service.   In a great many instances, letters have been returned with some miserable, contemptible expression written by a miserable southern sympathizer in regard to the service they have entered, probably stating that their families do not require relief, or information from such contemptible "trash."

Under such circumstances, it would be extremely unsafe to forward money to their families, for the reason that it will fall into the hands of those who are wholly unprincipled and would benefit no one.

From my knowledge of Kentucky slave owners, gained while

recruiting in the state, I can safely state that the above illustration is the rule and not the exception.   Men who plead with their lives in their hands are certainly worthy of consideration, without regard to color.   I have to request in behalf of the enlisted men of the Regiment, that some plan be adopted whereby such portion of their pay as they may see fit to set apart, may be placed in the hands of their families for their own use.

. . . .

HLcS   D. M. Sells[10]

> The disintegration of slavery seemed to intensify the violence on which the system had always rested. Frances Johnson, the wife of a soldier, experienced the expiring agonies of slavery as she struggled to liberate not only herself but also her three children.

Camp Nelson Ky   25th March 1865

Personally appeared before me J M Kelley Notary Public in and for the County of Jessamine State of Kentucky Frances Johnson a woman of color who being duly sworn according to law doth depose and say—

I am the wife of Nathan Johnson a soldier in Company F. 116th U.S.C. Infty.   I have three children and with them I belonged to Matthias Outon Fayette County Ky.   My husband who belonged to Mary Outon Woodford Co. Ky enlisted in the United States service at Camp Nelson Ky. in May 1864.   The day after my husband enlisted my master knew it and said that he (my husband) and all the "niggers" did mighty wrong in joining the Army.   Subsequent to May 1864 I remained with my master until forced to leave on account of the cruel treatment to which I was subjected.   On Wednesday March 8th 1865, my masters son Thomas Outon whipped me severely on my refusing to do some work which I was not in a condition to perform.   He beat me in the presence of his father who told him (Thos Outon) to "buck me and give me a thousand" meaning thereby a thousand lashes.   While beating me he threw me on the floor and as I was in this prostrate and helpless condition he continued to whip me endeavoring at one time to tie my hands and at another time to make an indecent exposure of my person before those present.   I resisted as much as I could and to some extent thwarted his malignant designs.   In consequence of this whipping suffered much pain in my head and sides.   The scar now visible on my neck was inflicted at that time.   After such treatment I determined to leave my master and early on the following morning—Thursday March 9" 1865 I stealthly started for Lexington about seven miles distant where my sister resided.   On my arrival there I was confined on account of sickness produced by the abuse I had received from my masters son as aforementioned.

During Friday March 10" 1865 I sought a lodging for myself and children—   Towards evening I found one and about 7 o'clock at night I left for my masters intending to take my children away.   About 9. O'clock I arrived there much fatigued, went to the Cabin where my children were, no one but the colored folks knowing that I was present, got my children with the exception of one that was too sick to move, and about 10" o'clock P.M. started for a neighboring Cabin where we remained during the night.   At day break next morning I started for Lexington.   My youngest child was in my arms, the other walked by my side.   When on the Pike about a mile from home I was accosted by Theophilus Bracey my masters son-in-law who told me that if I did not go back with him he would shoot me.   He drew a pistol on me as he mad this threat.   I could offer no resistance as he constantly kept the pistol pointed at me.   I returned with him to his (Bracys) house carrying my children as before   I remained at Bracys all day.   My sick child was moved there during the day.   I tried to find some chance of running away but Bracey was watching me.   He took my eldest child (about seven years of age) and kept her as an Hostage.   I found I could not get away from Bracey's with my children, and determined to get away myself hoping by this means to obtain possession of them afterwards.   I knew Bracey would not give me my children or allow me to go away myself so at daybreak on the following morning Sunday March 12" I secretly left Bracey's, took to the woods in order to elude pursuit, reached Lexington and subsequently arrived at Camp Nelson.   My children are still held by Bracey.   I am anxious to have them but I am afraid to go near them knowing that Bracey would not let me have them and fearing least he would carry out his threat to shoot me.   And further the deponent saith not

her

HDcSr   (Signed) Frances   Johnson[11]

mark

Even after emancipation had won the day in the other border states, slaveholders in Kentucky continued to fight tenaciously to keep freedom at bay. Enlistment in the Union army remained the only road to liberty for the state's slaves. When Congress adopted a joint resolution in March 1865 freeing the wives and children of black soldiers and future recruits,[12] slaves in Kentucky responded with a renewed surge of enlistments. Owners threatened volunteers and their families with violence, while local police and slave patrols redoubled efforts to obstruct the flight to recruitment centers. A soldier recounted how he and his wife had been foiled in their first attempt to escape.

Camp Nelson Ky   March 29, 1865

Personally appeared before me J M Kelley Notary Public in and for the County of Jessamine State of Kentucky William Jones a man of color who being duly sworn according to law doth depose and say—I am a soldier in the 124th U. S. C[*olored*]. Infty.   Before enlisting I belonged to Newton Craig   Scott County Ky   My wife belonged to the same man.   Desiring to enlist and thus free my wife and serve the Government during the balance of my days I ran away from my master in company with my wife on Saturday March 11th between nine and ten Oclock at night.   Our clothes were packed up and some money we had saved from our earnings we carried with us.   On our way to Camp Nelson we arrived at Lexington about Three Oclock next morning Sunday March 12" 1865 where we were accosted by the Capt of the night watch James Cannon, who asked us where we were going.   I told him I was going to see my daughter   He said I was a damned liar, that I was going to Camp Nelson.   I then told him that I was going to Camp whereupon he arrested us, took us to the Watch House where he searched us and took our money from us taking Fifty eight (58) dollars from me and eight (8) dollars from my wife.   I told him that the money was my own that I desired to have it,   He told me that he would send it with the man who would take us back to our master and when we got there we should have it.   I said I would rather die than go back to master who said he would kill any of his niggers who went to Camp. Cannon made no reply but locked us up in the Watch house where he kept us all that day and night and on Monday morning March 13" 1865 he sent us back to our master in charge of an armed watchman whose name I believe was Harry Smith.   When we arrived at my masters master was away from home and Smith delivered us to our mistress.   I asked Smith to give me my money.   He said Cannon had given him none

but had kept the whole to himself.   I ran away from home that day
before master came home.   I have never received a cent of the money
which Cannon took from me.   I have three sons and one son-in-law now
in the service of the United States.   I want to get my money back.   And
further Deponent saith not

his

HDcSr   (Signed) William   Jones[13]

mark

> To escape abusive owners and obtain freedom, hundreds of sol-
> diers' families fled Kentucky and sought refuge in Ohio River
> cities like Cincinnati and New Albany, Indiana. A black resident of
> New Albany informed the secretary of war of the refugees' hostile
> reception.

New Albany. Ind.   April 1st 1865

Sir. I. H. G. Mosee. take my pen in hand to inform you of the hardships
and troubles of Colored Soldiers Wives here.   it makes my heart bleed to
see how they are treated.   some are starving   some are robbed out of
all their poor husbands leave for them   those persons are the so called
Contrabands.   they have made their way to this place and no Men with
them or the greater part of them   the most of them have come from
Kentucky   We, the Colored people of this place do all we can to help
these poor people and I thought by applying to you that we would be a
great deal better off if such Conduct could by any means be prevented
if one Colored Man had Military Orders to see after such persons this
would be stopped.   such as Kidnaping and carrying Soldiers Wives and
Children back into Kentucky and going into their houses stealing what

they have and because the Colored Women have not got a White Witness they cant do any thing   they can stand and look at their own property but cant get it because they have no White witness or Military Man to speak in their favor.   as fast as Contrabands come they will take him and put him in jail and tell him he cant get out unless he goes as a Substitute and sell him for one thousand. dollars and give him one hundred or one hundred and fifty.   they tell him they will give him five hundred dollars until he is Mustered in and then pay him what they please.   he may have a Wife and Children then they will say to him give me your Money and I will give it to your Family or I will give you fifty dollars and carry the balance to your Family but not a dollar will the Family get and so they go   I cant tell you (sir) how bad it is   I know you will put a stop to this and if you will give me orders I will go any length for such poor people.   I was licensed by J. H. Almy. to recruit for the. 29th and 30th Regiments of Colored Volunteers.   I will send you my license and you can see what I have been doing.   you will please to return them to me again.   and if your (Honor) will send me such papers I will be pleased to serve for the Benifit of the Colored population of this place.   if ever the poor Colored people wanted a Beaureau* it is here.   your humble servant

ALS   H. G. Mosee[14]

Other families of black soldiers remained at home, awaiting the men's release from military service and anticipating their reunion as free people. But the end of the war did not mean that slavery

---

*A reference to the Bureau of Refugees, Freedmen, and Abandoned Lands (Freedmen's Bureau), which had been established through legislation approved on March 3, 1865. The bureau was charged with supervising the transition from slavery to freedom in the former slave states. (*Statutes at Large*, vol. 13, pp. 507–9.)

was abolished in Kentucky. Not until the ratification of the Thirteenth Amendment in December 1865 did slavery officially come to an end.[15] In the meantime, state authorities enforced the slave code with vigor and refused to acknowledge the validity of the congressional resolution freeing soldiers' families. In such circumstances, it was difficult for the women and children to find employment or even a place to live. When the Reed family sheltered Jane Coward and her children, Coward's former master and an accomplice pursued them, beat her brutally, seized the oldest child, and issued murderous threats against the wives of black soldiers and anyone who harbored them. Coward appealed to her soldier-husband for retribution against her attackers.

Green Cty   Ky.   July the [6] 1865

Dear Husband   i set my self down to write you a few lines to let you know that Mr Reed twoke to me and my three children to live with him to live and R. L. Moor and Mr. Frank Coward come hear to day and beat me nearly to death   he says that he will kill any man that will take me in to a house to live with him   Pharoah this is roat by Sarah M Reed* i want you to hand this to your captain Stranger   i want to know of all you that is a friend to the cullard people that you have got thar husband in survice i want you to come to greens burg and treat old Coward just like he did Pharoah wife to day   and he said that if i said one word that he would searve me the same way   he knocked hear down and old dick more hell hear and Coward beat hear nearly to death   he took the older girl with him home and he said to jane that before she should live with me he would killer de[ad] and all of the Reeds that was on top of earth in less than one weak   i would ceap you wife but R L more

---

*At this point in the letter the voice changes from that of Jane Coward, wife of the black soldier Pharoah, to that of Sarah Reed. The latter, who penned the letter, was evidently the wife of the Mr. Reed who had taken in Coward and her children.

says that he will kill every woman that he knows that has got a husband
in the army   he said that i was no better than a negro rage and i think
that i am just as good as he is   i never treated nothing as he did
Pharoah wife to day   i want you to come to greens burg and let me see
you and tell you all about it   i think we will have to leve hear on the
acount off the rebels that is hear for if a man ever leaves his wife and
children at home by thar selves thay are abusded by some one of
them   you must do some thing for Mr Frank coward in return to his
treatment to day to Pharoah wife   i never was so abused in my life by
no man   my husband is not at home to day   i have two children in the
uion army and we have two children that was killed in the union army
and i think that aught to have some peace at home when my husband
leaves me at home   do pray do come to our relieaf at home   nothing
more but this   your wife

jane coward

rote by Sarah M Reed[16]

HLSr

Letter from soldiers in the 1st U.S. Colored Cavalry
to a War Department official. (See pp. 129–130)

CHAPTER

V.

SOLDIERS' FAMILIES AND THE POSTWAR ARMY OF OCCUPATION

OR BLACK SOLDIERS AND THEIR FAMILIES, the war changed everything. The Confederacy had been defeated, the master class vanquished, and slavery destroyed. As part of the victorious army, black men were eager to share the fruits of the Union's triumph with family and friends from whom they had long been separated. Like other soldiers, they saw opportunities aplenty in the new America that the war had created. But for black men and women, the end of the war presented possibilities that white soldiers and their families could never imagine, for it promised previously unknown security and advancement.

Realizing freedom's promise, however, was not an easy task. If at times the war seemed to have changed everything, at other times it seemed to have changed nothing. Again and again, former slaves found their most profound aspirations frustrated and their hopes and plans dashed by the refusal of the old order to exit gracefully. Nothing angered a black soldier as much as learning that his family was "[l]iven . . . just as much Slave as the[y] was . . . before the war broke out."

Black soldiers in the postwar army of occupation felt both the possibilities and the frustrations that attended the arrival of freedom. As representatives of the Union, they placed their authority in the service of their people, attending political conventions, building schools, sponsoring orphanages, adjudicating disputes, and serving as advocates and counselors. Their confidence, armed presence, and knowledge of the world beyond the plantation allowed them to advise and protect those struggling to find a way from slavery to freedom in the postemancipation South. Yet, the very circumstances that propelled black soldiers into the role of liberator and protector often prevented them from fulfilling their responsibilities to their own families and sometimes placed them in harm's way.

Federal authorities generally mustered regiments out in order of their enlistment, with the first in being the first out. Since black men entered the army late in the war, they were among the last to be released. Black soldiers squirmed uncomfortably as they watched white comrades exchange their uniforms for civilian garb, return to their families, and take up the task of remaking their lives. Envy turned to outrage when news arrived that families and friends had been assaulted by former owners and other Confederate revanchists.

Several circumstances compounded the soldiers' anger. As white soldiers were discharged, black regiments made up a growing proportion of Union troops in the defeated Confederacy; the postwar army of occupation was blacker than the army that fought the war. Federal officials worried about the effect of black soldiers on the expectations of the former slaves, and white southerners insisted that the presence of black soldiers undermined efforts to maintain order. Such concerns resulted in the removal of many black regiments to distant parts of the South, far from the centers of black population. Thousands of black soldiers were sent to the Texas border to guard against the threat of French imperialism in Mexico. When pleas from family and friends who had been evicted, abused, and exploited reached these distant posts, the fury of black soldiers could hardly be contained.

The federal government itself contributed to the abuse. To encourage enlistment, the government had promised to protect and support the soldiers' parents, wives, and children. For many such people, support came in the form of rations, shelter, and protection in "contraband camps." With the war's end, federal officials were eager to reduce governmental expenditures by terminating the distribution of rations and disbanding the camps. In the process, they conveniently forgot the origins of these entitlements and violated almost every pledge the government had made. The soldiers' faith in their own government was further compromised by the behavior of officers who failed to accord wives and parents the respect soldiers believed was their due.

The postwar violence against the families of soldiers and the withdrawal of promised governmental support brought howls of protests from men who still wore their country's uniform. It intensified the freedpeople's desire to place their families on a firm footing.

General E. O. C. Ord, the newly appointed commander in tidewater Virginia, was not squeamish about circumventing the government's pledge to support the families of black soldiers. When he found that northern public opinion would not allow the simple termination of rations, he searched for some way to put black women to work. Rehearsing the narrow range of domestic occupations open to black women, Ord smugly lit upon a solution.

Richmond, Va., May 12th *1865.*

General.   In reply to your note on the subject of issuing rations to families of negro soldiers, I have to reply that it is not deemed proper to stop the issue suddenly by any general order, simply because it might raise a cry at the North, but you can issue orders to the various superintendants to open intelligence offices, in each, to gather the unemployed women and hire them out, and in case no means of employment offers, to try and find work for them, as nurses to hospitals, to make clothing or wash for prisoners, or for the other negroes, detail them as laundresses for the Companies of the 25th Corps in the field, and send them to the

Companies where they have, or claim to have husbands, or if every other source of labor fails, gather these women and children into buildings and open a grand *general* washing establishment for the city, where clothing of any one will be washed gratis.

A little hard work and confinement will soon induce them to find employment, and the ultra philanthropists will not be shocked.   Very Respectfully Your Obedient Servant

HLS   E. O. C. Ord[1]

> Roanoke Island, a small spit of land off the coast of North Carolina, had been set aside to house the families of black soldiers recruited in tidewater North Carolina and Virginia. Because the island was crowded and could furnish only modest gardens, its residents— almost all of them women, children, and disabled or elderly men— depended on rations from the federal government to make ends meet. The reduction of rations created a crisis on the island. William A. Green, an army chaplain and military superintendent of freed-people, and several missionaries who were stationed on the island asked the commissioner of the Freedmen's Bureau to intervene.

Roanoke Island. N.C.   June 5" 1865

General   In behalf of suffering humanity which it is not within our power to relieve, we appeal to you trusting that the necessity of the case may be sufficient reason for addressing you personally and directly

There are about thirty five hundred blacks upon this island, the larger part of whom are dependents of the following classes, viz.   Aged and Infirm, Orphan children and soldiers wives and families.   Of these about twenty seven hundred have (including children) drawn rations from the Government, and by this assistance and the exertions of benevolent Societies they have been cared for, though not without extreme suffering in many instances up to the present time.

Those who are able to work have proved themselves industrious and would support themselves, had they the opportunity to do so, under favorable circumstances.   The able bodied males with few exceptions are in the army, and there are not many families on the Island that have not furnished a father, husband or son, and in numerous instances, two and three members to swell the ranks of our army.   And these left their families and enlisted with the assurance from the Government that their families should be cared for, and supported in their absence.

The issue of rations has been reduced, so that only about fifteen hundred now receive any subsistence from the Government.   The acre of ground allotted to each family has been cleared and tilled, to the best of their ability—but this has only produced a very small part of what has been, and is required for family consumption.

We know that it is not the design of the government to support those who will not work, in idleness, nor is it the wish of those who make this representation as this would [be] an evil not Second to slavery itself

Nor is it to complain of the spirit of the government towards this unfortunate class, but to state the facts of their condition as they exist and bespeak such assistance as humanity shall dictate to the infirm and helpless, and such support as may be justly claimed for the families of soldiers whose wants the Government is bound to supply until they can be placed in a position to be able to Sustain themselves.

If it is the design of the Government to return these families to their former masters to be supported and cared for by them, this design has not been explained to them, and no facilities have been afforded them to leave the island, while the sweeping reduction of the rations brings hundreds suddenly face to face with starvation.

There are numerous cases of orphan children who have been taken in, and afforded a shelter while subsistence was furnished, who are now cast off because they have nothing to eat.

There are many who are sick and disabled whose ration has been cut off, and these instances are not isolated, but oft recurring and numerous.　It is a daily occurrence to see scores of women and children crying for bread, whose husbands, Sons and fathers are in the army today, and because these things are fully known, and understood by those whose duty it is to attend to, and remedy them and disregarded by them. we appeal to a Source more remote and out of the ordinary channel.

We do this with a feeling that the emergency demands immediate action to prevent suffering which justice, humanity, and every principle of christianity forbids

With the hope of immediate investigation which Shall bring with it a Speedy relief, We remain Your Obt Ser'ts

W^{m} A Green	Susan Odell
Caroline A Green	Mrs. R. S. D. Holbrook
Amasa Walker Stevens	Ella Roper
Mrs S. P. Freeman	E. P. Bennett
Esther A. Williams	Kate L. Freeman[2]

HLS

Black soldiers with families on Roanoke Island also protested the mistreatment of their wives, children, and parents. Enlisted under the promise that their families would be fed and sheltered while they served in the Union army, they denounced the federal government's violation of its pledge and appealed to the commissioner of the Freedmen's Bureau on their families' behalf.

[City Point? Va. May or June 1865]

Genl   We the soldiers of the 36 U.S. Col[*ored*] Reg[t] Humbly petition to you to alter the Affairs at Roanoke Island. We have served in the US Army faithfully and don our duty to our Country, for which we thank God (that we had the opportunity) but at the same time our family's are suffering at Roanoke Island N.C.

1   When we were enlisted in the service we were prommised that our wifes and family's should receive rations from goverment. The rations for our wifes and family's have been (and are now cut down) to one half the regular ration. Consequently three or four days out of every ten days, thee have nothing to eat.   at the same time our ration's are stolen from the ration house by Mr Streeter the Ass[t] Sup[t] at the Island (and others) and sold while our family's are suffering for some thing to eat.

2nd   Mr Steeter the Ass[t] Sup[t] of Negro aff's at Roanoke Island is a througher Cooper head* a man who says that he is no part of a Abolitionist. takes no care of the colored people and has no Simpathy with the colored people.   A man who kicks our wives and children out of the ration house or commissary, he takes no notice of their actual suffering and sells the rations and allows it to be sold, and our family's suffer for something to eat.

3rd   Captn James the Suptn in Charge has been told of these facts and has taken no notice of them.   so has Coln Lahaman the Commander in Charge of Roanoke, but no notice is taken of it, because it comes from Contrabands or Freedmen   the cause of much suffering is that Captn James has not paid the Colored people for their work for near a year and at the same time cuts the ration's off to one half so the people have neither provisions or money to buy it with.   There are men

---

*I.e., "copperhead," a northerner who supported or sympathized with the Confederacy.

on the Island that have been wounded at Dutch Gap Canal, working there, and some discharged soldiers, men that were wounded in the service of the U.S. Army, and returned home to Roanoke that Cannot get any rations and are not able to work, some soldiers are sick in Hospitals that have never been paid a cent and their familys are suffering and their children going crying without anything to eat.

4th our familys have no protection the white soldiers break into our houses act as they please steal our chickens rob our gardens and if any one defends their-Selves against them they are taken to the gard house for it. so our familys have no protection when Mr Streeter is here to protect them and will not do it.

5th. Gen[l] we the soldiers of the 36 U.S. Co Troops having familys at Roanoke Island humbly petition you to favour us by removeing Mr Streeter the present Asst Supt at Roanoke Island under Captn James.

Gen[l] prehaps you think the Statements against Mr Streeter too strong, but we can prove them.

Gen[l] order Chaplain Green to Washington to report the true state of things at Roanoke Island. Chaplain Green is an asst Supt at Roanoke Island, with Mr Holland Streeter and he can prove the facts. and there are plenty of white men here that can prove them also, and many more thing's not mentioned   Signed in behalf of humanity

Richard Etheredge
Wm Benson[3]

HLS

Although fair in principle, the demobilization of regiments in order of their organization left a disproportionate share of black soldiers under arms, since full-scale black recruitment had begun only in 1863 and continued well into 1865. As white soldiers returned home to their loved ones, the government shipped black soldiers to the Rio Grande border to counter the French-backed monarchist forces that had seized power in Mexico. The commander of a black cavalry brigade described the circumstances that had driven his men to mutiny on the eve of their departure from Virginia.

[*Brazos Santiago, Texas   June 1865*]

. . . .*

The majority of the 1st and 2[d] Regt[s] USC[*olored*] Cavalry are residents of Portsmouth & Norfolk & vicinity, and the 2 USC[*olored*]. C[*avalry*]. having met their families and Children (nearly 1000 as I am informed) they were unwilling to leave them unprovided with money or rations.   Consequently they became excited and decidedly insubordinate.   At which juncture Major Dollard Comd'g instead of being with his men on shore to rule and prevent outrage, retired to the Cabin of the Steamer and some time after called the Line Officers away from their Commands, probably for consultation thus leaving the men on shore unrestrained by their presence.

During the excitement some (20) twenty Men deserted and left with their families, but in a few hours order was restored and the leaders of the Mutiny I took from the Boat—placed in irons, and have them in custody

All the men appearing contented before seeing their families, and even afterward promptly obeyed all orders in arresting their comrades but were enraged at the threat of using white troops to coerce them, as was offerred by Major Dollard 2[d] USC[*olored*]. C[*avalry*].—

---

*The first page or pages are missing. The events described in the surviving portion of the letter took place as several regiments from the 25th Army Corps, recently shipped down the James River to Norfolk, Virginia, awaited embarkation for Texas.

I found the same feeling of discontent and insubordination in the 1s Regt USC[*olored*] Cavalry. Many were wishing to see their families and being unable to make any provision for their support from not having been paid and rations having been stopped to Soldiers wives—

Major Brown, Comd'g 1" USC[*olored*]. C[*avalry*]. while this state of affairs prevailed left his Command and was absent at Norfolk all night leaving his Arms on the dock at Fort Monroe, and his Troops in charge of his subordinate officers who found it necessary to shoot (not fatally) one man and turn over to me six more whom I ironed.

With the exception of Major Brown 1" USC[*olored*] C[*avalry*] and Major Dollard 2 USC[*olored*]. C[*avalry*]. the officers of the Brigade both Staff and Regimental were all prompt and dutiful, and for their close attention to duty, and sober, earnest labor in the prompt and thorough embarkation of this Command, (no boat being detained an hour) they merit my warmest thanks, not one being behind time or neglecting an order a course of conduct which if pursued by their superiors would I am convinced have prevented any disturbance whatever, for every man left Camp as cheerfully as ever before.

I should have placed both Major Brown and Major Dollard in arrest but for the apparant encouragement to the insubordinate enlisted men—

I have mentioned the condition of the families &c not as an excuse for the conduct of the men but showing the cause of the excitement and the stupidity of permitting them the inflamatory stimulus of free intercourse with the howling multitude—

We arrived at Mobile Bay the 23^{d} inst having had a smooth voyage of seven (7) days where (Fort Morgan) we found orders to proceed to Brazos Santiago, Texas.

A Report of the voyage from Mobile Bay to Brazos Texas will be

forwarded as soon as practicable.   I remain Very Respectfully Your
Obedient Servant

HLfS   Geo. W. Cole[4]

> Six months later, news reached the Virginia soldiers that their fam-
> ilies had been denied all assistance. Already dissatisfied with their
> transfer to Texas, they became desperate to be discharged. In a let-
> ter to an unnamed official in Washington (probably the secretary of
> war), they offered to buy their way out of their remaining service in
> order to return home to care for their families.

Brazos Santiago   Texas,   Dec 1865
Sir   here is my Compliment & wishes to be pertectd by the War
Department
    1st U S Colred Cavalry   sir Wee present to you our sufering at
present Concerning our Famileys wich wee are now informed that
Commisserys has been Closed a gainst them as though wee were
rebeling a gainst U S. and has Came to be a great Wonder & a great
Contemplation a mung the men of this regt and wee would be happay to
find some one to pertect us in thes Case   Wee have been on Dayley
fetig from the Last of Juli up to this Day without a forlough or any
comfort what ever & our wifes sends Letters stateing thir suferage
saying that they are without wood without wrashions without money
and no one to pertect them   Wee have Done the best that wee can do
and trys to obey orders and would pleassed to know the Cause of our
Dishonorble in treatment   Wee have been exspecting to be musered out
of the Army. Why because wee knew the men wich wee have taken for

our friends was acquinted with what Liberty. wee have been granted up
to this time and for that cause wee thought that it would please any good
hearted man to turn us out of servis to the pertecttion of our be loved
wifes   and if there be any man North or south Let him say to Day
what shell be our pertecttion for this Day wee Disiaer to know.

here wee have come in as U S. Soldiers and are treated as
Slaves   never was wee any more treated Like slaves then wee are now
in our Lives   I well remember before the Closeing of the war that men
who was fighting a gainst the U S. how thir wifes were pertected and if
our wifes were half pertected as they were wee would be happy men.
Wee are said to be U S Soldiers and behold wee are U S Slaves   Wee
are now well acquinted with earley riseing and Late bed time and such
things wit wich has been don here of Late is a shame to. be. don before
the men of the south

Wee had rather pay for our next years serviss and be turned out then
to stay in and no pertecttion granted to our wife

Sir wee would be verey much pleased to be Dis banded from the field
and if the War Department Can not spar us or spar the time. wee. will.
pay them for one years. servis. in the beside what soldiering wee have
done   Wee onley wish the pertecttion of our wifes and as we has been
all ways been so acomodated with the Law for any thing that wee do
young [*wrong*] wee now wish to be comodated for what wee have done
right   and if I have said any thing young I pray to be exc[*used*].   your
obeient U S Servts

also wee cant get a forlough unless paying $60 Dollars and wee thinks
verey hard of it[5]

HL

While black soldiers struggled to return to their families, wives and children faced former owners—many of them embittered Confederate veterans—without the protection of their husbands, sons, and brothers. Indeed, former Confederates singled out for special punishment the families of black men who had contributed to their defeat. Letters like these from the wife and sister of a Louisiana soldier informed black soldiers of the trials their families faced in the old Confederacy.

Roseland Plantation [*La.*]   July 16th 1865

My Dear Husband   I received a letter from you week before last and was glad to hear that you were well and happy.

This is the fifth letter I have written you and I have received only one— Please write as often as you can as I am always anxious to hear from you.   I and the children are all well—but I am in a great deal of trouble as Master John Humphries has come home from the Rebel army and taken charge of the place and says he is going to turn us all out on the Levee unless we pay him (8.00) Eight Dollars a month for house rent— Now I have no money of any account and I am not able to get enough to pay so much rent, and I want you to get a furlough as soon as you can and come home and find a place for us to live in.   and besides Amelia is very sick and wants you to come home and see her if possible   she has been sick with the fever now over two weeks and is getting very low— Your mother and all the rest of your folks are well and all send their regards & want to see you as soon as you can manage to come— My mother sends her compliments & hopes to see you soon

My children are going to school, but I find it very hard to feed them all, and if you can not come I hope you will send me something to help me get along

I get all the work I can and am doing the best I can to get along, but if

they turn me out I dont know what I shall do— However I will try &
keep the children along until you come or send me some assistance

Thank God we are all well, and I hope we may always be so   Give my
regards to all the boys.   Come home as soon as you can, and cherish me
as ever   Your Aff wife

HLSr   Emily Waters[6]

.

Roseland Plantation [*La.*]   July 30th 1865

My Dear Brother   I learn by Hannibal that you are well and happy—
Mother and all the rest of us are well but we are in deep trouble— Your
wife has left Trepagnia and gone to the city and we dont know where or
how she is, we have not heard a word from her for four weeks

Master John has come home and is going to turn us all out of doors
unless we pay him $3.00 per month rent, and we have no way to earn the
money and it is coming mighty hard on us   David has left and gone
some where— He has been gone over two weeks and we dont know
what has become of him—

My little boy has been very sick, but is getting quite well now—
Moses is well and sends his regards,   Aunt Rosalie and Aunt Liddie
both send their love & best wishes

Moses wants you to send him a pair of soldiers pants if you can—
Hopeing to hear from you soon   I am Your Aff Sister

HLSr   Alsie Thomas[7]

> An officer of the company in which Waters's husband and
> Thomas's brother was serving reported their case to the Louisiana
> headquarters of the Freedmen's Bureau, explaining that their
> grievances were widespread occurrences.

Fort St. Philip. La. Aug. 1st, 1865.

Sir. I am an officer in a co. of 140 men.—have been with them
continually Since their organization as a Co., and most of the time the
Sole officer with them. Feeling an interest in the advancement and
prosperity of the colored race and always sympathizing with them in
their trials and Sufferings, which are now very great, owing to the
peculiar condition of the country, and their people, those under my
immediate charge have learned to look to me for consolation in regard to
many matters not Strictly military. I always do what I can but
frequently that is nothing at all. One of the most frequent complaints
brought to me is the mistreatment of Soldiers wives, and in Some cases
their ejectment for non-payment of rent by *returned rebels* who seem to
be resuming their old positions all over the country. This of course is
inhuman as well as contrary to Genl. Orders. No. 99. H^{d} Qrs. Dept. of
the Gulf. June 30th, 1865, which declares that the families of Soldiers in
the Service of the Gov't. either on land or water, Shall not be ejected for
rent past due, and no collections of rent forced until further orders.
This is a very humane provision but owing to the ignorance of many
colored persons it is *very* often violated. Those who know of the
provision do not know how to go to work to receive their rights under it,
frequently, and when they do attempt it they are often snubbed by those
who they feel a right to expect as their friends. Truly, the colored race
are passing through an ordeal that will test every virtue they possess,
and it will not be astonishing if, in many cases they fail to meet the
expectation of an uncharitable world.

My object in writing you this letter is to call your attention to a Mr.
John Humphrey, who I am told is a returned rebel officer, now living on
Roseland Plantation, St. Charles Parish, who is Said to have made
innumerable threats and at least one attempt to put out the family of

Contraband camp at Hampton, Virginia. (*Harper's Weekly,* Sept. 30, 1865)

one of my Soldiers.—*for non-payment of rent.*— I gave the man a
furlough and he got home Just in time to find a *Provost Guard* at his
house for the purpose of ousting his wife and children.   These look like
Strange proceedings viewed at this distance with my understanding of
the law.   The fact is, persecution is the order of the day amongst these
returned rebels, against the colored race in general, and Soldiers
families *in particular*.   And I am grieved to Say that many wearing the
U. S. uniform are too easily bought body and Soul over to the evil designs
and purposes of these same individuals.   It seems to me that your
Bureau and its agents are the "forlorn hope" of the colored people.—
These rebels Strongly object to these agents, and declare that they will
only keep up a confusion and disturbance, continually.   That means
that they do not intend to manifest the "good faith" for which Genl.
Howard* hopes, but intend to take Such a course with the colored
people as will *oblige* the interference of the agents of your Bureau.

   These are my views, although I owe you an apology for expressing
them at Such length.   If it pleases you I shall be glad to lay the frequent
cases which arise in my Co. before you, as I know your voice is very
potent   With great respect I am Your Most Obt. Servt.

ALS   Hugh P. Beach.[8]

   Life away from family was as hard on those left at home as it was
   on those who marched off to war. The worried wife of a black soldier from New York informed her husband of their son's dangerous
   illness.

---

*Oliver Otis Howard, commissioner of the Freedmen's Bureau.

McGranville [*N.Y.*]　July 26th [*1865*]

My Dear Husband　　I received a letter from you to day. and was vary
glad to hear of your good health, and also that you had received two
letters from me.　but Oh Husey I have sad news for you　　littel Fay is
vary sick　　he was taken sick tusday morning had a vary hard stumake
ake didnot eat hardley any breakfast but he begd so hard for me to let
him go to school that I concented but I have been vary sory that I
did.　when he got home from school he never eat any super and went
wright to bead　　he said he was sick all over　　I give him some P S
[*Townsdson?*] sasuprilea and thought he would be better in the morning
but befor dark he was taken out of his head　　I had hard wourk to
keeap him in the bed talking evry thing you could think of with . . .*
feaver and vometed and bowel complaint　　in the morning he was no
better　　Mr Forshee was going up to Cortland and I toled him to tell Dr
Ball to come and see him　　he got [*here*] wendsday about three Oclock
he said he was a vary sick boy.　he said he must not eat anything but
water porudge　　you must not wory to much about him　　he is not
dngrious yet and I hope he will be better in the morning.　but Oh how I
wish you could be hear　　Fay wants you to get a furlou and come home
just as soon as you can.　you say in your last letter that thear is no
order for the 54 to be musterd out.　Dr Hendrick said thear was an
order the day after you left for the 54 Reg to be musterd out imeadetley.
and Bill was up hear tusday and he said the same　　I thought you was
on your way home　　wall I must close　　I shall have to tend to
Fay.　may the Lord be with you and keep you in all your ways.　the rest
of us are well　　write soon

[*Etta Waters*]

---

*Corner of letter torn; one or two words missing.

[*In the margin*] and may the Lord hasten you home.   be faithuf to God
and tell them littel Orphen bosy of Jesus.   E. A.[9]

ALI

> The conflicting demands of family and military duty frustrated
> black soldiers who were eager to reassume their familial responsi-
> bilities. When their wives were abused by callous and corrupt offi-
> cers, the soldiers' anger boiled over. An anonymous letter from a
> Kentucky soldier to the secretary of war suggests something of the
> standards of treatment black soldiers expected for their loved ones
> and for themselves, along with the roles they expected to play as
> husbands, fathers, and sons.

Bryant Station   Lexington Ky   Oct the 22. 1865
Mr E M Stanton   We are here and our wives and children are laying
out doers and we have no chance to get a home for them   we havent
had Six days furlough to See our wives and we have been in the army
fourteen months   these officers are laying here and learning us
nothing   instead of them learning us Something they are Robing us
out of our money   they are taken our rations and Selling them and are
Keeping the money   i think it is mighty hard for us to Stand that after
just coming from under bondage   their are men that has never had the
chance to learn anything   they will give them change for a one dollar
for a fifty dollars in Stead of teaching them better   that is the way they
treat them.   we come in three years or Sooner discharge.   we would be
willing to Serve three years longer   under these circumstances it would
disheartin any one and haf to pay thirty dollars for a ten days
pass   when our wives comes to the camp to See us they are not allowed
to come in camp and we are not allowed to go and See them   they are
drumed of[f] and the officers Says go you damed bitches   you know

that it is to much they are treated So by these officer   they ought to be
a friend to us and them to   the major makes his Brages that he will
keep these dam niggers in until he makes a fortune   they have us
cleaning up farms and cutting up Stumps for these citizens and they pay
the officers for it and they are allowing these citizens to run over us   if
we Say anything to them we are put in jail and two or three months pay
docked from us   if you please to allow us the privelege of going home to
Situate our familys for the winter   we hate to See them laying and
Stroling around but we cant help our Selves   we are able to Situate
them by labor if they will allow us the privelege   we have payed nine
hundred dollars for the rasing of our brass band   now they want to
claim the instruments off of us   its now more than what i masters
would have done   the lost of this fifth regiment is over thirteen
hundred dollars by these officers   i think it is mighty hard for us to lay
here and they fool with us that way and when they here of us being
mustered out they Says that they will right to washington and they will
holde us   they Say if they cant holde us any other way they will move
us out of the State   Shame Shame Shame how we are treated   they
will not let us trated out Side of the Sutlers   if we do they want to
punish us   things that the Sutler has got that is onley worth a dollar
they charge us Seven or eight dollars   if you want to by anything out
Side they Say know god dam you go to the Sutlers and by

   I must bring my letter to a close   5. U. S. "C[*olored*]." Cav[*alry*]
your most devoted Soldier until death[10]

HL

> Having escaped slavery and endured the constraints of military
> life, soldiers were eager to take their places with their families, gain
> access to land, and exercise their rights as free men. Military ser-

vice became unbearable as they saw those possibilities slip away. Once gone, soldiers from South Carolina informed a federal commander, these lost opportunities would place them at a permanent disadvantage.

Morris Island   So Ca   January 13 1866

My Dear Respictfully Friend General Sickels   it is with much Honor we take to write to you about the Circumstances of our case   now Genl do if you please Cir to this lookin to this [for us].   now General the Biggest Majority of our mens never had a Home Science this late war Commence between the States   the Greatist majority of them had Runaway from they Rebels master & leave they wives & old mother & old Father & all they parent   jest Run away from they Rebels master in the years 1862. & 1863 & come Right in under the Bondage of Soldiers life living & according to agreement & promised we was expected to get out at the Closing of the war, & then go back over the Rebels lands to look & seek for our wives & mother & Father

But General now to see that the war is over & our Enlisment is out the Greatist majority of by two months & the General characters of our Regiment we do not think that the our Goverment have knowit   for Instant I think if he had know the General characters of our Regt he would let us go at the Closing of this [*war*]   for instant look & see that we never was freed yet   Run Right out of Slavery in to Soldiery & we hadent nothing atall & our wifes & mother most all of them is aperishing all about where we leave them or abbout the Country & we hear on morris Island Perishing sometime for somthing to Eate   Half of our money got to use up in the Regtal Sutler for somthing to Eate & we all are perrishing our self & our Parent & wives all are Suffering

& do General if you Please do see & Enterceed & see if you cannot do

any good to get us out of this if you please cir   for all other Colored
Soldiers that had a Home & is well situated at Home is go back but we
that never had a Comford Home we is heer yet & we will have to buy our
lands & places & by the time we get out of this all the Goverment cheap.
Property & all the lands that would sold cheap will be gone & we will
have a Hard struggle to get along in the US   & then all the Southern
white Peoples will have us for alaughin & game after for our Braverist
that we did to Run away from them & come asoldiers   they will be glad
to see that we would not have but very little money & we would not have
any land, atall for all the cheap in things are going now   So do Gen you
is the only one that we know could do any good for us beside forwarded
to Washington.   So Please if you can do any good for us do it in the
name of god   itis a mejority of men of the 33 Regt USCT[11]

HL

> Opportunities lost included not merely land, employment, or politi-
> cal advance. Long-standing ties unraveled as men and women sep-
> arated by time and distance established new relationships. The
> saga of Norman Riley, a Kentucky soldier, and his wife Catherine
> suggests how continued separation could dissolve deep ties of affec-
> tion.

Nashville Tenn   Aug 12th *1865*

Dear wife   I Received your letter that was writen on the 8th to day and
was glad to hear that you was well and that the children was well also.   I
am well as to health and well Satisfide all to Seeing you and as I can't
tell when I can come to see you my wishes is for you to come and See
me   I am in earnis a bout you comeing and that as Soon as possiable

it is no use to Say any thing a bout any money for if you come up here
which I [*hope*] you will it will be all wright as to the money matters   I
want to See you and the Children very bad and my love for you and the
Children is as great to day as it ever was.   I can get a house at any time
I will Say the word So you need not to fear as to that   So come wright
on just as Soon as you get this.   I also wish you to get George to give
you Some money to bare your exspences here.   and if you cant get off
you must write to me a gain and I will try and Send you Some
money   I want you to tell me the name of the baby that was borm
Since I left   that is if you can't come up here.   and I want you to bring
my son George with you for I want him.   and if it Suits you you can
leave your daughter Elisabeth there with George.   I am your
affectionate Husband untill Death

Norman Riley

Write Soon[12]

ALS

Nashville Tenn   Aug 26 *1865*

Dear and affectionate Wife   I Seat myself to write you a few lines to
let you know that I am well hoping that these lines may fine you the
same.   Dear wife I would like you to come down if you Possible can   I
wrote to you some time a go to come and you did not come and I dont
know the reason for I have not got any letter from you to hear how you
was nor to know cause of you not comeing.   I cant tell when I shall get
out of service and I want to See you very bad and if you [*want*] to See
me you will have to come and see me and I would like for you to come for
I think that you can make a great deal more here then you can.   and
you George I think very hard of you for not coming and Seeing me for
you know that I cant come and See you and therefore you ought to come

and See me and if you dont feel like coming down here I want [*you*] to come and bring my family and you can go back if choose.

now if you cant come I want you to write me an answer to this as Soon as you Receive it.   I have Nothing more at Preasent but I Remain Your Most affectionate Husband Untill Death.

Derect your letter as headed above in care of Capt. F. P. meigs (Box 115)

Norman Riley

Write Soon   yes I have got a house all Ready for you and if cant come I Shall reant it out a gain in the coure of ten days so good by[13]

ALS

Clarksville Tenn   Aug 28. /65

Dear husband   It is with pleasure that I Seat myself for the perpose of Writing you afew lines.   acknoklage the recept of your letter. which came to hand in Dew time. it finding [*me*] very Well as I trust this may find you.   I am sorry to Inform you. that your brother George is very badly Wonded   he went out After my things and Jessie Boyd also.   Jessie went with him.   he was also shot. but not so bad as Geo.   and George wants that you should come down To see him if you posible Can. do so   he thinks that if you cannot come now. you Need not to come at all for he is very badly wounded   I guess you would like to know the reson why that I did not come when you wrote for and that is because that I hadnot the money and could not get it.   and if you will send me the money. or come after me I will come   they sent out Soldiers from here After old Riley. and they have got him in Jale In Bolling Green K.Y. and one of his Sons. Kernealious I think. was woulded by the Colord Soldiers. and they have his brother Elias here in Jale.   dear husband If you are coming after me. I want you to come before it Get too cold. that I cant Travel   I dont want you to Rent that house out. for if there is a better chance to make a living there. then what there is here. I want to get up there.

George was badly Shot through the Back.   the shot still remains in him and Jessie boyd was shot through the thigh.   I seen Uncle Moses Riley. Sunday and he told me to give you his best respect. and tell you that he was well and doing very well.   dear husb I havenot got my things from home yet but I shell. as soon I can.   having nothing more to Write. I shell close hopeing to hear from you soon   I Remain as ever your affectionate and Loving Wife

ALS   Catherine Riley[14]

                           Nashville Tennessee   Sept[r] 22nd *1865*

Mr Dear Wife   I again the pleasure of writing to you To let you know that I am In the enjoyment of Good health.   I would like to know the reason why you did not answer my last two letters.   I am very anxious to hear from you. and particularly to know if you are coming Here.   if you are coming I would like for you to come immediately, as there is A man here about. to buy a house and he has no person to go into it to take care of the things.   also let me know if George has got well or not   I am very anxious to hear from him   I want you to write to me inside of an hour after you receive this and let me know what you are going to do   I will now conclude hoping to hear from you son   I remain your affectionate & Loving Husband

HLSr   Norman Riley[15]

> Unwilling to join her husband until she had rescued their child, Catherine Riley sought the assistance of a Freedmen's Bureau agent in Clarksville, Tennessee. In a letter to the chief bureau officer for Kentucky and Tennessee, the agent described what happened when she tried to claim the child.

Clarksville Tenn   Decr 19. 1865

Sir   I have the honor to call your attention to the following statement
and ask your advice thereon

On the 9th ult I gave Catherine Riley, the wife of a soldier, an order to
James Riley of Logan Co Ky. for her child which the said Riley still
claimed as his Slave.   She got the child & started on her return to this
place & when about three miles from said Rileys, he overtook her, & did
unlawfully beat her with a club, & left her senseless on the ground after
which he returned home with the child.   Catherine Riley reported to me
the following day. and substantiated the above facts by competent
witnesses & at the time was all covered with blood. could scarcely talk &
was barely able to stand alone.   The above facts have also been told to
me by a neighbor of the said James Riley—   I sent a guard for him but
he could not be found, as he had gone from home & taken the said child
with him, as he remarked. to a neighbor, to "put the child out of the
reach of the d——d Yankees   Not long since this same man Riley
shot a negro soldier, & ran away from home to prevent his being
arrested.

Cases of the above kind are reported to me about every day, but many
of them I cannot attend to on account of not having soldiers to enforce
my orders at a distance

I respectfully refer this matter to you & ask your advice thereon
Resp^{ct} Your ob^t Servt

ALS   W. G. Bond[16]

Bond's successor as Freedmen's Bureau agent in Clarksville later
reported that James Riley was arrested, tried, and fined $100 for
having "maltreated" Catherine Riley.[17] But as she struggled to lib-

erate their child, her husband—perhaps impatient about her delay
in joining him—found solace in a new relationship. Catherine Riley
made out the following affidavit against her husband, who mean-
while had been discharged from military service.

State of Tennessee   Montgomery County   5 day of May 1866
Catherine Riley being duly sworn and examined on oath makes
complaint & says that Norman Riley late of Logan Co. Ky & the slave of
John Riley in the fall of 1856 did marry this affiant according to the
forms & ceremonies practiced among colored people and her the said
Cathrine then & their had for wife.   That affiant has had four (4)
children by him three of whom are now living.   That she has ever been
faithful in marrige relations.   And that the said Norman Riley
afterwards and while he was so married to this affiant as aforesaid to
wit in the year 1865 at the City of Nashville in the State of Tennessee he
the said Norman Rily feloniously & unlawfully did marry & take to wife
one other colored woman whose name is unknown to this affiant—this
affiant his former wife being then & now living, against the power &
dignity of the State & contrary to the forms of the Statute in such case
made & provided—
  Wherefore affiant prays that he be arrested & dealt with according
to law

her
Catherine ✕ Riley
mark

[*In the margin, in another handwriting*] This man works at Roaring
Springs Ky.   This is such a flagrant case that it is desirable to send this
to Gen Fisk—   Will Dr Cobb please swear this woman & send this to
Gen Fisk.

[*In the original handwriting*]   5' day of May 1866

    Affiant further says that she presented the above affidavit to Dr Cobb
Bureau Agent of the freedman here who refused to swear her to it.   She
further says that the above affidavit is true & she prays that Gen Fisk
will help her.   She says that Dr Cobb told her that if her husband when
arrested should swear that the children were not all his, it would send
this affiant to State Prison

                                                                  her
HDSr   Catherine × Riley[18]
                                                                  mark

        Asked to explain his refusal to accept Catherine Riley's affidavit,
        Joshua Cobb, the Freedmen's Bureau agent at Clarksville, revealed
        the erroneous genetic assumptions that caused him to believe she
        was lying about her children's paternity.

                                     Clarksville [*Tenn.*]   May 24th 1866
    Respectfully Returned with the following statements—   That
sometime in April last the colored woman in question (Catharine Riley)
made to me substanially the statements contained in the paper herin
enclosed marked A.—   But knowing that some of Catharines children
were bright mulattoes, and some quite black, I could not see how she
could sustain these statements and would advise her with the letters (the
same herin enclosed) and a letter which I would give her, to go before the
Supt of the Bureau at Cadiz Trigg County Ky who would have her
husband brought before him, and then face to face, with her the
difficultly could be settled.   I saw no more of Catharine until, about the
5th of Apl—when she came to my office with the paper marked A. drawn

up by or in the office of Messr Buck & McMullin, with a request from them that I should sware her as to the statements therein contained but on reading over the paper I was convinced that it would be improper for her to make oath to the same—and stated to her that should she do so she would lay herself liable to prosecution for perjury   And here I would state that Doctor A. C. Swartzwelder of your city being present and his attention being called to the case after asking the woman (Catharine) a few questions—became himself convinced from her answers that it would be wrong for her to be sworn to the statements contained in said paper—and that further in a few hours after this—the Doctor and myself in making a visit to the contraband camp—happened to call at the cabin occupied by said Catharine and her children—and the Doctor's attention was called to the Mulattoe & Black children of said Catharine, all of whom she was about to and has since sworn to be the children of Norman Riley—and the Doctor then & there told her it would not do for her to sware to the Statements of said paper   The next I heare of the matter is on the receipt of the enclosed papers from your office with request to report on the facts and from which I learn that the simple woman, from advise of her lawyer—went before the County Court clerk and made oath to the correctness of the contents of said paper—   I have only to add that I know of no better way to adjust this matter than the one herin already suggested by me to the woman Catharine   all of which is respectfully submitted

Joshua Cobb[19]

AES

> If some soldiers abandoned old relationships for new, others contin-
> ued to yearn for dear ones at home. The emotional strain of separa-
> tion suffused the letter of "an umble soldier" to the secretary of
> war.

Wives and children welcome mustered-out black soldiers. (Pencil drawing by A. R. Waud, Library of Congress)

Helena Ark   May. 15th 1866

Dear Sir   I imbrace this opertunity of writing you a few lines to inform
you that I am well at present hoping those few lines may find you
engoying the same gods blesing   I am a soldier of the 56th Colerd
Infintry under Col— Benzona and have preformed my duty as a soldier
should   since I inlisted I have never ben abesent at eny rool call   I
inlisted January the 4th 1864 under Col Russel Culumbia boon County,
Mo. when I left my family I promised them that I would come home on
furloe   in August last I lost two of my children   I asked for a leaf of
absence and was refused   thare has ben but one man furloed in my
comand and he was qtr master sargent and that was this year   in my
redgement we have a large magority Christians and I thank god for
it   thare has ben a grate meny of my felow soldiers who throgh grief
and anziety about their families have pined away and died   there has
severl Redgements who inlisted one year after we did mustered out and
gone home   we stood on the bank and shed teers to think that we who
had batled for our country over two years should still be retained and
deprived of the priviledge of seeing those who are so dear to us   my
actions have proved that I have ben true to my government and I love it
dearley   now the war is over and I now want to see those who are
dearer to me than my life   thare is a great many of my Brother
Soldiers who have ben out since the first Battle was faught in mo and
have never seen their families   I have nothing more to say   hoping
that you will lend a listening ear to an umble soldier I will close

ALS   James Herney[20]

For the men of a Kentucky regiment, the struggle to balance the "great and Noble coas" that had ensured freedom and their duty to "our Wifes and our homes and children" defined much of African-American life for themselves and future generations. The war for freedom, for domestic integrity, and for black nationality was of one piece.

Whites Ranch   Texas   May 30 1866

Sir   I has the orner this morning to adress a few Lines to you Consuring the condishion of our Famuleys of Kentucky.   a humble Good and faiful Soldier.   the few remarks I wish to say is this   the condishion of our Famuleys at home sum of them are Suffren for wanting of healp and Needing of retention.   and reson Why I Wish to inform of this. is because that. I Know that my own Famuley is Liven in old Kentucky under just as much Slave as the was when I left her or before the war broke out.   and agreat mani of other Men's Famuleys is Liven the Same Life.   Now M[r] President and Ceterry. When we in Listed in this great and Noble coas. we did not heasertate the Least. But we came out like Men and Stud with in the feeal. with Vengengs againts the amny in-ten-erley [*intending?*] to eather to ful-fil our Dutys and to obay all orders that was agreable to Millerterry or to the regerlation of the United States en if not for victry so we did intended to waided in Blood upto our chins.   Now M[r] President and Ceterry. we all can Say this much and we do not Say it just for a Prise nor for a large Name here after. for every word that is Spoken in this Letter is true.   the 116. U. S. Col.[d] Regiment She has don. her duty, and i thinks cording to the regerlations that is gaven by the House of Congress of War we has ben Prompest to all dutys in the feeal or on Picket dutys or Girson or fertig or any other dutys that may be Put before us. and I dont think the quarters is Shorn to us that is intended for us. it is very true thire has ben furlowes easherd [*issued*]. but a Mighty few of them. What has ben easherd they was easherd to the Men that the Officers Like the best. and the good and duble [*dutiful?*] Soldier had to Stand Back. thire is agreat Parshalege Shored in among the Men out here. thire was a few furlowes easherd to 116 US Col Inf. about 17th of this. month and I dont think it was don justis. f[*or*] thire was only two men a lod out of a Company of the 116. Regiment. U. S. Col Inf. and we has not any way to send our Money home   the men that gos home they lives in adifrent part of the State. and thire is no Purson that we could trust for we has sent large amounts of Money to our famuleys. and they has not got it.   and I larns that thire is a Numbers of our famuleys has ben turned out of Doors, and they has no Place to lay thire heads and we has no way to healp them.   Now Mr Prisident and Ceterry I think that a duble Regiment as we has ben and has Prove it to the World. and then to have nomore quarters Shorn to us then what has ben I dont think it is right. it is true that all Soldiers Should obay all orders wich the 116. Regiment. U. S. Col Inf. has don ever Sence we has in the feeal.   Only one thing I surpose you know all about it that happen at city-point of. V.a.* but you know how that is.   Where thire is a hundred Sheaps thire must be a Black one.   But this is what Pleas me. is this   we has Stud up like men Man for Man. in the time of action in the feeal of. V.a. and Never has flench nor Dreded the time up to this Present moment.   M^r

---

*In May 1865, at City Point, Virginia, two sergeants of Company I, 116th U. S. Colored Infantry, led a group of soldiers in refusing to serve any longer under their captain because he customarily punished the men by tying them up by the thumbs. The sergeants were convicted of mutiny and executed. (Proceedings of general court-martial in the cases of Sergeant Doctor Moore and 1st Sergeant William Kease, 18–19 May 1865, MM-2394, Court-Martial Case Files, Judge Advocate General [H-37].)

President and Ceterry. aflet a moment to think what a Condishion we
Kentuckys. came out upon the Condishion that we Left Our Famuleys
in. yest. But the way was oping that is very true. that we Poore Nation
of a Colered rast Might come out in our Native State to afend for our
Selfs and the Next Generration to come. See how willely we come. and
Left our States our Wifes and our homes and children in such away that
they may do the best they can and to take cire of thire Selfs. ye. what
kind of fixt was it to. Now the old Servent he has no Propty he has no
Money he has no House to put them in to. What is they to do now when
they is turn out of House and home. I would like to Know how would
they go about takeing cire of thire Selfs and Children. when this Poore
old Soldier had nuthing to leave with them. No House to put them in
to. the old Servent has Spent the best of his days in Slavery. then
must these Poore Creatchers be Sufferd to lye out of Doors Like Beast
or sum brute. I says No. if our Govener is for us a Poore unhapy
Soldier Wich has Stud. with Comrights to comrights. and Sholder. to.
Sholder Marching Boldly in the feeal. And then Suffer his Soldiers
Famuleys and Piarints. to Suffer with Such Punishment is that   I
thinks not. Now Mr President and Ceterry. you Need not to think that
we holds you all asponerbul [*responsible*]. for Such treatment for we do
not. We beleave the Govener is just. and if our feeal Offecers and
Company Commanders would use the Laws a corden to the Law of the
regerlations that is gaven to them by the House of Congress. why we
dont think that Such treatment would be don   and—Mr President. is it
Law-ful for a Company Offecers to Detail Men Soldiers. out of thire
Companys to wait upon them as a Servent. and Boot-blacker or a cook
and keep them. I dont think thire is any. Such law is that. in the
regerlations. and then at the same time gave them the Power to Punishe
them at the ful Extent as if a Genel cort marshel might Punish a Soldier

when he has don a great crime   Now Mr President and Ceterry I hope
that there is no harm in Doing this   I Shall Close   I remain your true
Beleaver and Well Wisher

	G. E. Stanford	John Dannlus
	W. P. Southwith	Mc Feedlins
HDSr	Mc Mear	William Berry[21]

Marriage ceremony of a black soldier and a freedwoman, Vicksburg, Mississippi. (*Harper's Weekly* June 30, 1866)

CHAPTER

VI.

HUSBANDS AND WIVES

HE CONJUGAL RELATIONSHIPS OF SLAVES HAD
no legal standing, no formal protection against intrusions
by the owner. Husbands and wives could reside together or visit
across plantation lines only with their owners' consent. They had
no recourse against sexual abuse. Their unions could be perma-
nently shattered at any time by the sale of a spouse or other forced
separation.

In the face of these circumstances, slaves forged their own
understandings of marriage, the proper regulation of sexuality, the
obligations of husbands to wives and wives to husbands, and the
role of the wider slave community in sanctioning and enforcing
such expectations. With the long-awaited end of slavery, they
adapted these understandings to the new world of freedom.

Eager to celebrate publicly relationships that under slavery had
received but backhanded and partial recognition, husbands and
wives validated their marriages before clergymen and government
officials. In so doing, they not only confirmed the arrival of freedom
but also established their unions at law and thereby gained the
claims to progeny and property that only legal marriage could

provide. Spouses who had belonged to different owners seized the opportunity to live together under one roof. Former slaves whose marriages had been broken by sale and distance set out to reunite with long-lost husbands and wives. Young men and women marrying for the first time created families free from the constraints that slavery had imposed. And if the validation of extant and new relationships was a mark of freedom, so was the dissolution of unwanted ties. Like legal marriage, divorce embodied the determination of black people to remake their world.

The creation and dissolution of marital bonds was only a small part of the reformulation of relationships between husbands and wives. Whether confirming longstanding unions or establishing new ones, men and women had to formalize the responsibilities that marriage entailed. Generally this process took place in the unstated affirmations of daily life. At times, however, some dispute—a violation of the marriage bed, a domestic conflict turned violent, contention regarding the custody of children—became the occasion to articulate the obligations of husbands and wives. As freedpeople delineated the standards to which they held each other—sexual fidelity, mutual economic support, responsibility for children and other kin—they both affirmed the legacy of the slave family and announced their aspirations for freedom.

The familial and sexual practices of the fugitive slaves who poured into Union lines during the Civil War received intense scrutiny from northern observers, especially the military officers and civilians who supervised the "contraband camps" established to house the refugees. During the fall and winter of 1862–63, General Ulysses S. Grant's Department of the Tennessee organized such camps at Corinth and Holly Springs, Mississippi; Lake Providence, Louisiana; Cairo, Illinois; and Memphis, Lagrange, Bolivar, Grand Junction, and Jackson, in western Tennessee. To obtain information about the former slaves, Chaplain John Eaton, Jr., the general superintendent of contrabands in Grant's command, circulated a questionnaire to the superintendent of each camp and compiled the responses for a report to Grant's headquarters. One of Eaton's "interrogatories" concerned the ex-slaves' understanding of marriage.

April 29, 1863.   Memphis [*Tenn.*].

.   .   .   .

Answers to Interrogatories.

.   .   .   .

INTERROGATORY 19   What of their marital notions & practices.

ANSWERS.

Corinth.   All wrong.   All entering our camps who have been living or desire to live together as husband and wife are required to be married in the proper manner, and a certificate of the same is given.   This regulation has done much to promote the good order of the camp.

Cairo.   Their idea of the marriage relations and obligations is very low.

Grand Junction   Most of them have no idea of the sacredness of the marriage tie, declaring that marriage, as it exists among the whites, has been impossible for them.   In other cases, the marriage relation exists in all its sacredness without legal sanction.

*Holly Springs and Memphis.**   The greater number have lived together as husband and wife, by mutual consent.   In many cases, strongly attached and faithful, though having no legal marriage.

Memphis.   They know what marriage is among the whites, but have yielded to the sad necessity of their case.   Generally, I believe the men to be faithful to the women with whom they live, and the women to reward their faith with like truth.   Free and married, they will maintain the marital relations as sacredly as any other race.

Bolivar.   Have had no opportunity for correct notions and practices.

La Grange.   Loose & by example.

Providence.   No answer.

.   .   .   .

HLcSr   (Signed)   John Eaton, Jr.[1]

---

*A contraband camp at Holly Springs, in northern Mississippi, had
  been abandoned when Confederate forces seized the post in December
  1862; its residents were moved to Memphis.

Ex-slaves held firm convictions about what freedom should mean. At the very least, they believed, the integrity of their families should no longer depend on the goodwill and fortunes of others. They therefore welcomed opportunities to place their personal relationships on legal footing. By the end of the Civil War, thousands of husbands and wives had reaffirmed unions established during slavery—often unions of long standing. In Mississippi, at Vicksburg, Natchez, and Davis Bend, army chaplains recorded more than 1,400 such marriages in 1864 and early 1865. The following page from the Vicksburg register includes entries for the new and renewed marriages of several black soldiers.

[Vicksburg, Miss. July-September, 1864]

Date	Name of Male	Place of Birth	Name of Female	Place of Birth	Age-Yrs.	Color										Name of Officiating Minister and Witnesses
1864. July 17	William Montgomery	K, 5th U.S.C.H.A.	Vicy Ann	Yazoo City, Miss.	23	Blk										Joseph Warren
" 25	John McQueeny	6th U.S.C.I.	Sarah James	Ill.	42	Mul.										Charles Warren
" 31	Wilson Martin	Vicksburg, Miss.	Mary Martin	Vicksburg, Miss.	73	"					16 free	20	Blk			1 free	Walter C. Young
" "	Henry Marshall	F, 53d U.S.C.I.	Hannah Marshall	"	51	Blk										E. Fuller, Parent
August "	Eldijer Mitchell	K, 51? "	Adelia Coleman	"	40	"			10			40				8 adults 1	Joseph Warren
" 4	Collins Morris	Vicksburg, Miss.	Susan Statham	"	24	"				1		17	Mul.	Mul.	Mul.	18 " 13	Henry Marshall "
" "	Eldijer Mitchell	See above										25	Blk	Blk	Blk	4 " 2	Riley Gordon "
July 10	Nat Martin	Bolivar, Miss.	Mary J. Lansbury	Carroll, So.	23	Mul.						19				1 "	Charles Gordon
" 31	Henry Miller	4/7th U.S.C.I.	Ann M. Chrisney	Lake Washington	49	"		6	"			229	Blk	Blk		1 China	Amanda H. Grist
August 14	John A. McCook	St. Cooper, So.	Saretta Harris	Vicksburg, Miss.	46	Blk	Blk	10	"			232	Blk	Blk	Blk	5 adults	G.W. Carrollton Walter C. Young Charlotte W. Buckley Louis Robinson
" 21	James Mullins	K, 5th U.S.C.H.A.	Margaret Taylor	"	20	"						25	"	"	"		2 S.H. Saylor, O.B. Hawtree
Sept. 4	Paul Wolf	H, 52d U.S.C.I.	Ann Mealy	"	39	"			1 free			140				7 free 2 6	Joseph Warren Charles Warren
" "	James F. Murphy	C, 11th U.S.C.I.	Cilla Ann Burns	"	21	"						21					Hannah B. Hawley Eliphas Wolf
" "	Aaron Weges	H, 52d U.S.C.I.	Anna Grun	"	21	"						119				11 adult	Thomas Eichbox Asa Merrill
" 11	Wesesd McDaniel	B, 52d U.S.C.I.	Harriet McDaniel	Washington Co., Miss.	21	"						11					Joseph Warren Maria Cathin John Warren Eliza Thomas

2

During the war, as throughout the long history of slavery, masters and mistresses honored their slaves' conjugal ties only if it suited their own convenience. When the owner of a black soldier's wife obstructed the couple's correspondence and pointedly affirmed that their relationship depended on his sufferance rather than their wishes, the soldier asked the secretary of war to overrule the master's arbitrary authority.

U. S. Gen. Hospital, Hampten, *V.A.*   January 26th 1865

Sir.   I the under-Sined, Respectfully ask for the liberation of my Wife and children now residing in the State of Ky. Boone County.

I enclose two letters Received from there   one is supposed to be from my Wife   the other is from a man claiming to be my Wifs master by the name of Jerry, *Smith.** You can see by the contents of his letter forbidding me not to write, Saying that he only gave her to me on my good conduct Of which he Says I have not fullfiled   it is not necessary for me to say anymore   you can see his letter,—

And as I am a *Soldier.* willing to loose my life for my Country and the liberty of my fellow man I hope that you will please be So Kind as to attend to this   please lett me know, or send me your Reply and oblige your humble Servent,   yours very Respectfully

ALS   Aaron Oats[3]

[*First enclosure*]   [*Union, Ky.*]   December the 22 64

Dar husban   I receive your letter dated December the 7 64 which gave me much pleasure to hear that you ar alive and well   I mus state that I and mother and the children ar all well hopping thet these few lines may still find you well still   I am at home and far as well as usial   I shall

---

*The two enclosures are in the same handwriting, presumably that of the master.

content myself and wait for the time to come as you thought you could not get a ferlough   I must state that there is another one was Born sence you left but I suppose you heard of it   if you have not I will tell you hernane is effis tell   [pood?] as they call him can run half as fast as you can and fat asever   your sisters ar all well   Johns mother states that, she wish that John would right and if he wont Right when you right again send all the perticklers About him whether he is live ordead.

N.B   you stated in your letter that you sent me too letters and your picture but I never receivd either

so I must conclude my short letter by saing that I send my love to you all and keep the Best part for your self   so no more till death

HLSr   Lucrethia[4]

[*Second enclosure*]   [*Union, Ky.   January 10, 1865*]

When your letter came to hand it was red and answerd and when I went to put it in the office ther was another at hand Equal as insolent as the other so I concluded to send you a few lines apon my own responsibelity and, not to wright any more with out you will have some Respect for me   ~~if you dont they will not be red nor answered~~   my darkes has too much Sence to be foold in such away   ther has been agreat menny woman and children have left and returned back again   one instant in my nabohood   Henry corben's mandy you nod her   dan had encoyd her and six children over in cincinnati out on walnut hill and there she and three children starved to death   the oldest that could travel came home and got his master to bring them home to keep them from starvation and too of the youngest had ate flesh of ther fingers   N B   Lucretia dont belong to you   I only gave her to you for wife dureing good behaviour and you have violated your

MARRIAGE LICENSE.

Bureau of Refugees, Freedmen and Abandoned Lands,

State of Kentucky, *Pendleton* County, *Oct 19th 186 6*

TO ALL WHOM IT MAY CONCERN:

The RITES OF MATRIMONY are permitted to be solmenized between *James*

L. Warner a free man of color, and *Cloa Coal*

a free woman of color, the requirements of the law having

been complied with.

Witness my signature as Superintendent of Freedmen, Refugees, &c.

A. J. Rheer

Sup't. Freedmen and Refugees, ——District.

Marriage license issued to James L. Warner and Cloa Coal. (National Archives) plede, my darkes olways tells me when they want to leve me they will tell me they say that if they ar to be deliberated they want it don honorable

this lettere was rote the 22 of December but taken it back to answer you my self I neglected to put it in the office till now this being the 10 of January 1865 But my darkes is as well now as they wer then and doing better than when you was hear now, they ar wated on when you was hear they had you to wait on so no more

HL

[*Jerry Smith*][5]

If northern ministers and teachers took special interest in formal-izing the marriage relations of former slaves, the freedpeople them-selves pressed for ceremonies that celebrated the new security of black family life and brought their most intimate ties into confor-mity with the standards of a free people. One army chaplain, attached to a regiment of black soldiers in Arkansas, reported that he spent much of his time conducting such ceremonies.

Little Rock Ark Feb 28th 1865

. . . .

Weddings, just now, are very popular, and abundant among the Colored People. They have just learned, of the Special Order No' 15. of Gen Thomas by which, they may not only be lawfully married, but have their Marriage Certificates, *Recorded*; in a *book furnished by the Government*.* This is most desirable; and the order, was very

---

*Adjutant General Lorenzo Thomas's order authorized "[a]ny ordained minister of the Gospel, accredited by the General Superintendent of Freedmen, . . . to solemnize the rites of marriage among the Freedmen." (*Black Military Experience*, p. 712n.)

opportune; as these people were constantly loosing their certificates.   Those who were captured from the "Chepewa"; at Ivy's Ford, on the 17th of January, by Col Brooks, had their Marriage Certificates, taken from them; and destroyed; and then were roundly cursed, for having such papers in their posession.   I have married, during the month, at this Post; Twenty five couples; mostly, those, who have families; & have been living together for years.   I try to dissuade single men, who are soldiers, from marrying, till their time of enlistment is out: as that course seems to me, to be most judicious.

The Colord People here, generally consider, this war not only; their *exodus*, from bondage; but the road, to Responsibility; Competency; and an honorable Citizenship—   God grant that their hopes and expectations may be fully realized.   Most Respectfully

ALS   A. B. Randall[6]

> Not all ministers and teachers tried to dissuade unmarried black soldiers from establishing families. On December 3, 1863, Henry M. Turner, a minister in the African Methodist Episcopal Church who was serving as chaplain of the 1st U.S. Colored Infantry, presided over the marriage ceremony of Rufus Wright, a North Carolina ex-slave who had enlisted in the regiment in July, and Elisabeth Turner, an ex-slave from Virginia. Their marriage certificate appears on the following page.

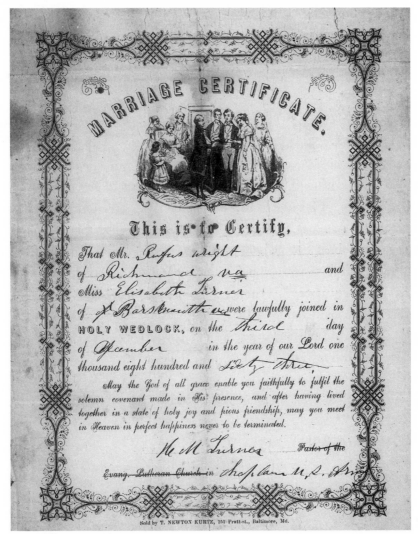

MARRIAGE CERTIFICATE.

This is to Certify,

That Mr. *Rufus Wright*
of *Richmond, Va* and
Miss *Elisabeth Turner*
of *Barsknith* were lawfully joined in
HOLY WEDLOCK, on the *third* day
of *December* in the year of our Lord one
thousand eight hundred and *sixty three,*

May the God of all grace enable you faithfully to fulfil the
solemn covenant made in His presence, and after having lived
together in a state of holy joy and pious friendship, may you meet
in Heaven in perfect happiness never to be terminated.

H. M. Turner Pastor of the
Evang. Lutheran Church in *Chaplain U.S. Army*

Sold by T. NEWTON KURTZ, 151 Pratt-st., Baltimore, Md.

7

In the months that followed their marriage, Private Wright wrote to his bride from various military camps, and they managed occasional visits, but their life together was destined to be brief. On June 21, 1864, his death from battle wounds made Elisabeth Wright a widow.

Camp 1st U.S.C.T. Near Hampton [*Va.*] apl the 2[2] 1864

My Dear wife   I thake this opportunity to inform you that I am well and Hoping when thoes few Lines Reaches you thay my find you Enjoying Good Health as it now fines me at Prisent   Give my Love to all my friend   I Recived you Last letter and was verry Glad to Hear fome you   you must Excuse you fore not Riting Before this times   the times I Recive you Letter I was order on a march and I had not times to Rite to you   I met witch a Bad mich-fochens I Ben [S]ad of   I Lost my money   I think I will com Down to See you this weeck   I thought you Hear that I was hear and you wood com to see me   Git a Pass and com to see me and if you cant git Pass Let me know it   Give my Love to mother and Molley   Give my Love to all inquaring fried

    No more to Say   Still Remain you Husband untall Death

                         Rufus Wright

Derect you Letter to foresess Monre VA[8]

ALS

wilson Creek Va   May 25th 1864

dear wife   I take the pleasant opportunity of writeing to you a fiew lines to inform you of the Late Battle we have had   we was a fight on Tuesday five hours   we whipp the rebls out   we Killed $200 & captured many Prisener   out of our Regiment we lost 13 Thirteen Sergent Stephensen killed & priate out of Company H & about 8 or 10 wounded   we was in line Wednesday for a battele But the rebels did

not Appear   we expect an Attack every hour   give my love to all & to
my sisters give my love   to Miss Emerline tell John Skinner is well &
sends much love to her.   Joseph H Grinnel is well & he is as brave a
lion   all the Boys sends there love them   give my love to Miss
Missenger   You must excuse my short Letter   we are most getting
ready to go on Picket   No more from your Husband

ALS   Ruphus Wright[9]

Norfolk [*Va.*] August the 21 1865

This is to certify That Elisabeth Wright Appeared Before me J W
Cook Notary and Counsiler Fore The Freedmen In This Department By
Permission Of Maj General Miles And Swore to The Fowling Statements
and the Said Testimony Was Confermed By Seargant Frank Turner 5th
Sergant Co [I] Wich Said Decased Belong to Captain William Brazzee
Col John Holman Commading Regiment 18 Armey Core Maj B F
Butler commanding   Having Stated That Her Husband Was Killed in
June 1864 Before Petterburgh Rufus Wright And She The Said
Widdow—Elisabeth Wright has Never Received Pay Or Allowances
From the Goverment And know Ask to Receive The Pay That May Be
Due The Said Rufus Wright Her Husband   I have The Honnor To
Remain Your Most Obedient Servant

Elisabeth   her mark ✕ Wright

Witness   his mark   Frank ✕ Turner

P. S.   The Papers in Testimony I here With Enclose To Be Retured with
you Convenience[10]

HDSr

With the end of the war and the abolition of slavery throughout the
South, greater numbers of freedpeople had opportunities to legal-
ize their marriages. Agents of the Freedmen's Bureau, which was
established within the War Department to supervise the transition

from slavery to freedom, were specially charged with helping former slaves take advantage of new marriage legislation adopted by
the various southern states. A Freedmen's Bureau superintendent
of marriages described his work in northern Virginia among soldiers of the 107th U.S. Colored Infantry and among black civilians
living in Freedmen's Village and other settlements of former slaves.

Freedmen's Village, Va.   June 1st 1866.

Dear Col: I have the honor to report to you concerning my efforts as
Supt. of Marriages in 5th Dist Va. from April 25th, to May 31st,
(inclusive) 1866.

My appointment from the Freedmen's Bureau, is dated April 18—
1866.   From that time to the 25th, I was so much engaged in closing my
obligations to the Philadelphia Committee of Orthodox Friends, relating
to several schools of Freedmen (Fort Strong, and other localities), that I
could give only a passing, and occasional notice to the marriage subject.

On the evening of April 25th, I preached on the subject of Marriage to
the soldiers at Fort Corcoran, 107. U.S.C.I. co. A & co E.   Capt. Goff of
co. A. and commander of the Fort, was present, and assisted me, by
reading the Circular on Marriage,* explaining it—and adding earnest

---

*Circular No. 11, issued on March 19, 1866, by the Freedmen's Bureau
  assistant commissioner for Virginia, quoted two February 17 acts of
  the Virginia General Assembly that gave legal standing to husband-
  wife relationships established during slavery and instituted
  procedures by which former slaves could obtain marriage licenses and
  have their unions legally recorded. The assistant commissioner
  instructed Freedmen's Bureau agents to "cause the above quoted laws
  to be read at all religious and other meetings of the colored people
  until they are sufficiently informed of the important change effected
  by legislation in their domestic relations." He also ordered bureau
  agents to register the names of former slaves who were "cohabiting
  together as man and wife" on February 17, 1866, and to "take pains
  to explain . . . that they are firmly married by the operation of the
  law." (*Black Military Experience*, p. 673n.)

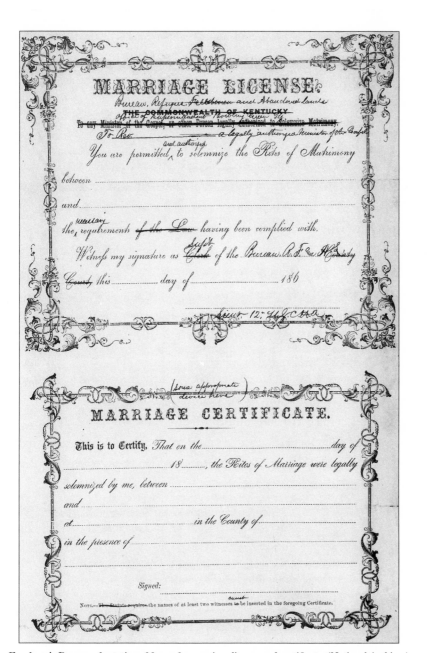

Freedmen's Bureau adaptation of forms for marriage license and certificate. (National Archives)

remarks, which exerted much influence on the minds of the soldiers. I record for him my *thanks* for such timely, and efficient assistance. I addressed the soldiers at that Fort several other times, on the same theme: these occasions included two Sabbath evenings. At the close of service on one of those evenings—Corporal Murray (of co A), said:—

"Fellow Soldiers:—

I praise God for this day! I have long been praying for it. The Marriage Covenant is at the foundation of all our rights. In slavery we could not have *legalised* marriage: *now* we have it. Let us conduct ourselves worthy of such a blessing—and all the people will respect us— God will bless us, and we shall be established as a people." His character is such, that every word had power.

I have preached & lectured, or *talked* publicly five times at Freedmens Village. From Apr 26 to May 30th, gave fifteen certificates: six to soldiers of 107 USCI Fort Corcoran; three to 107. Vienna Fairfax county— one-107 Freedmens Village— one 107 Alx——; and four couples of citizens, all of Alexandria co. Nearly three weeks of sickness prevented me from accomplishing more. Yesterday, 31st of May, we gave seventy nine certificates in Freedmens Village. We have much more to do. Rev R S Laws, Rev D A. Miles & lady teachers, much help me. Spent last Sabbath with Capt Ross, of Vienna & the way is open for work in that region. Yours

ALS   J. R. Johnson[11]

For some former slaves, freedom meant not an opportunity to con-firm marriages established during slavery but a chance to end undesirable unions. Perhaps these unions had been forced on the parties by their owners or by other circumstances of their enslave-ment. Or perhaps they represented formerly meaningful ties that had fallen victim to any of the innumerable difficulties besetting intimate relationships. The repudiation of such slave marriages did not, however, entail the abrogation of family connections. Instead, reported a local Freedmen's Bureau agent to the bureau's head-quarters in Florida, it created conflicting claims regarding the custody of children.

Lake City, Fla.   Oct 1 1866.

Sir,   The Act establishing and enforcing the Marriage Relation between persons of color passed by the General Assembly and approved by the Governor of Florida in January last, provides in what manner freedpeople who were living as man and wife before emancipation and *who mutually desire to continue in that relation* shall legallize their marriage, but fails to prescribe how cases are to be disposed of wherein the parties are opposed to being regularly joined in the bonds of matrimony.

I have had brought to my notice numerous cases of the latter Kind and would beg leave to quote the following, viz: Madison Day and Maria Richard, both colored, where living together as man and wife for seven years,   during that time three children were born the oldest of whom is now about six years of age.   Both husband and wife refuse to legallize their relation and both claim the children.   I have carefully investigated the case and find that neither party has any plausable reason for wishing to live apart from the other, nevertheless both appear to be determined to do so.   I must confess that I am at a loss to decide which of the two is to have the children or what disposition is to be made of the children.   Neither husband nor wife seem to be in a condition to provide for the children in a manner better than is usual with the freedpeople, still both appear to have an affectionate regard for the children and each loudly demands them.

I will thank you to lay this case before the Assistant Commissioner for the State of Florida for his consideration and decision.   I am, Sir, Very Respectfully Your obedt Servt

ALS   F. E. Grossmann[12]

> The assistant commissioner's ruling—"the father of the children shall have control of them"—enforced a common-law principle that by mid-nineteenth century had generally lost ground to judges' determination of a child's best interests and assumptions about women's special capacity for childrearing.[13]

> Because slavery had denied legal standing and protection to the slaves' family relations, marriage in conformity with the laws of civil society constituted a special emblem of freedom and respectability. The enforcement of legal marriage was therefore a matter of concern to the entire community.

Bladenboro   Bladen Co. N.C.   July 29 [18]67
Sir   The Colored people of this place are trying to make their colored bretheren pay some respect to themselves and the laws of the country by making them pay some respect to the marrage bond and stop the slave style of living to gather without being married.   there is one case in perticular they wish instruction   A colored man has been promising to marry a girl for the last year has been bedding with her most of the time They have had four times set for marriage but at each time he has but her of[f] with some excuse.

The colored men of this place appointed a committee to wait on him and see if they could not influence him to do better but no satisfaction could be obtained   Pleas write what course to pursue in such a case as this.   Very Respect.

ALS   J. E. Eldredge[14]

For thousands of former slaves, the new legal status of black family relations was of little significance unless they could locate and reunite with spouses, children, and other kin from whom they had been separated by sale or a master's migration. All across the South, freedpeople set about the task of reconstructing families fragmented by centuries of captivity. Philip Grey, a Virginia freedman, successfully searched out his wife Willie Ann and their daughter Maria, both of whom had been taken to Kentucky many years before. Willie Ann's affection for Philip and her wish that she and Maria might rejoin him were clouded, however, by concern about his willingness to accept her three children born since their involuntary separation, children now fatherless because of her second husband's death in the Union army.

Salvisa Ky · April 7th 1866

Dear Husband   I seat myself this morning to write you a few lines to let you know that I received your letter the 5 of this month and was very glad to hear from you and to hear that you was well   this leaves us all well at present and I hope these lines may find you still in good health.   you wish me to come to Virginia   I had much rather that you would come after me but if you cannot make it convenient you will have to make some arrangement for me and family   I have 3 little fartherless little girls   my husband went off under Burbridges command and was killed at Richmond Virginia   if you can pay my passage through there I will come the first of May   I have nothing much to sell as I have had my things all burnt so you know that what I would sell would not bring much   you must not think my family to

Bladenboro Bladenbo

July 29 67

Agt. Freedmans Bureau
Wilmington N.C.
Sir
The
Colored people of this
place are trying to make
their colored brethren
pay some respect
to themselves and the
laws of the country by
making them pay
some respect to the
marriage bond and
stop the slave style
of living to gather without
being married. There
is one case in particular
they wish instruction

Letter from J. E. Eldredge to to the Freedmen's Bureau agent

A colored man has been promising to marry a girl for the last year has been bedding with her most of the time They have had four times set for marriage but at each time he has put her of with some excuse of this place

The colored men appointed a committee to wait on him and see if they could not influence him to do better but no satisfaction could be obtained of less write what course to pursue in such a case as this.

Very Respect.

J. E. Eldredge

at Wilmington, North Carolina. (See pp. 172–173)

large and get out of heart for if you love me you will love my children and you will have to promise me that you will provide for them al as well as if they were your own.   I heard that you spoke of coming for Maria but was not coming for me.   I know that I have lived with you and loved you then and I love you still   every time I hear from you my love grows stronger.   I was very low spirited when I heard that you was not coming for me   my heart sank within me in an instant   you will have to write and give me directions how to come   I want when I start to come the quickest way that I can come   I do not want to be detained on the road   if I was the expense would be high and I would rather not have much expense on the road   give me directions which is the nearest way so that I will not have any trouble after I start from here   Phebe wishes to know what has become of Lawrence   she heard that he was married but did not know whether it was so or [*not*]   Maria sends her love to you but seems to be low spirited for fear that you will come for her and not for me.   John Phebe[*'s*] son says he would like to see his father but does not care about leaving his mother who has taken care of him up to this time   he thinks that she needs help and if he loves her he will give her help   I will now close by requesting you to write as soon as you receive this so no more at present but remain your true (I hope to be with you soon) wife.

Willie. Ann. Grey
To Philip. Grey

Aunt Lucinda sends her love to you   she has lost her Husband & one daughter Betsy   she left 2 little children   the rest are all well at present.   Pheby's. Mary was sold away from her   she heard from her the other day   she was well

Direct your letter to Mrs Mollie Roche Salvisa Ky[15]

ALS

Overcoming wartime separations could also be difficult, especially when erstwhile owners employed force and threats of violence to prevent former slaves from controlling their own families. When John Berry, a black soldier from Virginia, returned from the war and tried to claim his wife and children, he discovered that his participation in fighting for freedom had infuriated his old master.

Alexandria [*Va.*], Aug. 11/65

John Berry of Alex^a Va., vs. Benjamin Triplet of Fauquier, near Ashby's Gap, Va.   Complaint of refusal to allow him to bring away his family and of threatening his life as follows:

Berry states that on Monday the 7th inst. he went to Triplets, who said he went to the d——d yankes to fight against him—told him that the war was not over yet—that the niggers were not free.   He asked him for his family, but Triplet told him he should not have them—that nobody should take them away, and that if anybody come into the yard he would shoot them.   Berry has wife and 6 children from 4 to 14 years of age.[16]

HD

While it granted new security to black domestic life, legal marriage also changed the circumstances of conflicts between husbands and wives, introducing as it did both the law's protections and its restrictions.

State of Georgia   County of Chatham   24th day of July 1866

Personally appeared before me, "Capt J. Kearny Smith. A[*ssistant*]. S[*ub*]. A[*ssistant*]. Com[*mi*]s[*sione*]r" one Rosa Freeman"

"Freedwoman" who upon oath states that her husband (David Freeman "Freedman" to whom she has been married about nine months) has

Moore

Salvisa, Ky April 7th 1869

Dear Husband

I seat myself this morning to write you a few lines to let you know that I received your letter the 5 of this month and was very glad to hear from you and to hear that you was well this leaves us all well at present and I hope these lines may find you still in good health. you wish one to come to Virginia I had much rather that you would come after me but if you cannot make it convenient you will have to make some arrangement for me and family I have 3 little fatherless little girls my husband went off under Burbridges command and was killed at Richmond Virginia if you can make pay my passage through there I will come the first of May I have nothing much to sell as I have had my things all burnt so you know that what I would sell would not bring much you must not think my family to large and get out of heart for if you love me you will love my children and you will have to promise me that you will provide for them as well as if they were your own. I heard that you spoke of coming for Maria but was not coming for me I know that I have lived with you and loved you then and I love you still every time I hear from you my love grows stronger. I was very low spirited when I heard that you was not coming for me my heart sunk within me in an instant

Letter from Willie Ann Grey

you will have to write and give me directions how to come I want when I start to come the quickest way that I can come I do not want to be detained on the road if I was the expense would be high and I would rather not have much expense on the road give me directions which is the nearest way so that I will not have any trouble after I start from here Phebe wishes to know what has become of Lawrence she heard that he was married but did not know whether it was so or Marion sends her love to you but seems to be low spirited for fear that you will come for her and not for me, John Phebe son says he would like to see his father but does not care about leaving his mother who has taken care of him up to this time he thinks that she needs help and if she loves her he will give her help I will now close by requesting you to write as soon as you receive this so no more at present but remain your true (I hope to be with you soon) wife William Ann Grey

To Philip Grey

Aunt Lucinda sends her love to you she has lost her Husband & one daughter Betsy she left 2 little children the rest are all well at present, Phebe's Mary was sold away from her she heard from her the other day she was well

Direct your letter to Mrs Mollie Roche Salvisa Ky.

to Philip Grey. (See pp. 173–176)

beaten her repeatedly, and refuses to support her. we lived at Fernandina Fla— about four months— during that time he beat and abused me. I reported it to the Officer in charge of the Freedmans Bureau; he had him arrested & he got out of the *Guard House* & left the place, remaining away until a new officer took charge— he (my husband) then came back & beat me again— I had him arrested— he knocked the officer down & ran away & came here to Savannah. this in May 1866. since that time he has abused me & refuses to pay for the rent of my room & has not furnished me with any money, food or clothing. I told him that I would go to the Freedmans Bureau— he replied—damn the Freedmans Bureau—I'll cuss you before them. On Saturday night—he came to my room, took all his things, some four linen sheets & Some under clothes belonging to me & tore up two nice dresses of mine— he told me he would rather Keep a woman than be married—because she could not carry him to law & I could. I then told him that if he wanted to leave me—to get a Divorce & he could go— he said if I can get a Divorce without paying for it; I'll get it for you, if I can't I wont give it to you; you can go without it— I said if you want to leave me; leave me like a man! He has no just cause for complaint against me.

her

HDSr   Rosa × Freeman[17]

mark

Catherine Massey, the wife of a black soldier, shared Rosa Freeman's assumption that a husband's obligations to his wife included such material support as housing, food, and clothing. Massey's complaint about her spendthrift husband also revealed, however, that she regarded that obligation as mutual; wives, too, were expected to make material contributions to the household. She addressed her letter to the secretary of war.

Hampton   Fortress Monroe   Va   July 10th 1865

Respected Sir   I pen you this pamplet of a letter praying your honor to so arrange my Husband William Massey (Colored. 1st U. S.C T Com. G. Infantry) Money that when he is discharge I may receive Sufficient to meet my wants   I am his lawful wife and he has neglected to treat me as a husband should.   and unless your honor So arranges his money as to privelledge me to meet my wants, he never will as he is nothing but a Spendthrift   I have not received a cent of money from him Since last March /65—then he gave me twenty six dollars all of which he took back again   he has left me in detrimental circumstances and I know not how to meet my present wants   I have toiled and am still striving to earn my bread but as I feel myself declineing daily. I think it no more than right than that he should be made to do what he has never yet done and that is to help me to support myself as I helped yes not only helped but naturally did support him before he came in the army   I would not ask for any one to attend to his money matters for him. were it not for the fact that he seems to be to slothfull as to attend to it for him and myself   please attend to it for me and my prayers to Allmighty God for your honor shall be that God may prolong your life and enlarge your feild of good and at last when this mortal tenemant shall dissolve. prepare for you a mansion in the realms of unclouded day   With due respect to your Excellency I remain faithfully your Humble Colored Servant

Mrs Catherine Massey

When you Receive this please answer as soon as you can make conveneint   Direct thus Mrs Catherine Massey Hampton Fortress Monroe Va[18]

ALS

Sexual fidelity ranked high among the expectations slave husbands and wives held of each other, even when their unions had no legal standing. Kin, friends, and the wider slave community all condemned adultery. Jackson Fields, a discharged black soldier, thus justified his marriage to another woman on the grounds that his wife had been unfaithful while he was absent in the army. Denial of infidelity likewise sustained Sarah Fields's claim on her husband, on her own behalf and that of their child. Sarah Fields, Jackson Fields, and a witness all swore their affidavits before a Freedmen's Bureau agent in Louisville, Kentucky.

[*Louisville, Ky.*]   6" day of July 1866

Sarah Fields (colored) being first sworn says that she was married to Jackson Fields (a colored man) about three weeks before Christmas in the year (as she supposes) 1863   that she had one child by him in the regular time of nine months to first August 1864   That eleven months after the child was born her husband enlisted in the army— During all the time named they slept together without missing but very few nights   That the child spoken of above died in a short time after Jackson enlisted— That she now has another child by him which is about one year old— That she has Known no other man since they married   That she has remained in Woodford County ever since and learning that her husband after his discharge was living in Louisville Ky and she came down and on yesterday found him living with another woman to whom he says he has been legally married— She went to his house (situated in the suburbs of the city known as Limerick) and he would not recognize her as his wife and did not recognize the fact of his being the father of the child she alleges to be his but took hold of her and showed her off his lot into the street   That her husband enlisted in the month of October in the army

her

Sarah ✕ Fields[19]

mark

HDSr

[*Louisville, Ky.*]   6' day of July 1866

Jackson Field (colored) being sworn states that he enlisted in the
army in September 1864 and that he was discharged in April
1866   He says he did live with Sarah Fields as his wife before going in
the army and that he has not seen her since until yesterday   That after
he was discharged from the army he concluded to remain in Louisville

That he wrote one letter to Sarah while he was in the army and that
he got other soldiers who were writing home to their friends to say to her
as his wife that he was well—   He states that Susan Taylor a cousin of
Sarah came to the camp at Munfordsville to see her husband and told
him that his wife was acting badly and was living with another man
named John who then belonged to Mr Buford of Woodford
County   That after being in Louisville after his discharge he saw
another woman and asked her to marry him to which she consented and
he applied to the County Court Clerk of Jefferson County Ky and
procured a License and they were married and are now living together

his
Jackson ✕ Field[20]
mark

HDSr

[*Louisville, Ky.*]   7" day of July 1866

Susan Taylor (Colored) being first sworn says that she has been
acquainted for many years with Sarah Fields and Jackson
Fields   That she witnessed their marriage in the usual manner of
slaves marrying between three or four years since   that he continued
to live with her as his wife until he enlisted in the army

That she never heard any reports that Sarah was unfaithful to
Jackson during the time he was with her   that since he enlisted she
has heard it said that Sarah was unfaithful but she cannot say anything

of her own knowledge— She never witnessed any wrong conduct in
Sarah   That when she visited her husband while his regiment was at
Munfordsville she saw Jackson who was in the same regiment and he
asked her concerning the conduct of his wife and she answered that she
had heard that she was not doing right but she had not seen any wrong
conduct herself

her

HDSr   Susan ✕ Taylor[21]

mark

After hearing the case, the bureau agent gave judgment that Jackson Fields pay $50 to Sarah Fields "to assist in supporting her
child of which he is the father." Not satisfied with that decision,
Sarah Fields entered a complaint at the headquarters of the Freedmen's Bureau assistant commissioner for the state of Kentucky
(also in Louisville), swearing that her husband had deserted her
and married another woman, "and that she wants to get her husband back to help her make a living for herself and two children."
But when the assistant commissioner learned that the local agent
had already decided the case, he confirmed the earlier ruling.[22]

If allegations of adultery posed the most serious threat to relations
between husbands and wives, marital discord usually derived from
more mundane circumstances. One black soldier found the presence of his mother-in-law so disruptive that he sought the assistance of his company commander and the Freedmen's Bureau.

Fort Pickering [*Memphis, Tenn.*]   Decbr 20 1865
Major: Private Saml. Bolton of this Company wishes to lodge
complaint against his Mother-in-law, who is the alleged cause of much

trouble between himself and his wife.   He desires her to move out of his house and she refuses to do so.   Very Respectfully Your obt sevt

ALS   M Mitchell[23]

> The vast majority of former slaves were unable to rent or buy land to farm independently, and therefore had to hire themselves to planters as wage laborers or sharecroppers. They nonetheless struggled to reconstitute their work and family lives in ways that would reduce the direct supervision of white employers and allot more of the family's labor to self-directed activities. This struggle took many forms, including resistance to gang labor and overseers and the dispersal of the old slave quarters into separate family plots. A key component of the same process was the widespread withdrawal of black women—especially mothers—from field labor and their attention to productive activities at home. Planters were appalled by the consequent reduction in the labor at their disposal. One planter appealed to the head of the Freedmen's Bureau in Georgia for measures to require black women to return to the fields. Although couched as a means to prevent the impoverishment of the freedpeople, the planter's proposal revealed how crucial the field labor of black women had been during slavery, and it acknowledged the centrality of contests over family labor to the evolution of the new free-labor system. Indeed, as he warmed to the subject, the planter explicitly connected the question of controlling family labor to issues of labor discipline.

Snow Hill   near Thomson Georgia   April 17th 1866

Dear Sir— Allow me to call your attention to the fact that most of the Freedwomen who have husbands are not at work—never having made any contract at all—   Their husbands are at work, while they are as nearly idle as it is possible for them to be, pretending to spin—knit or something that really amounts to nothing for their husbands have to buy them clothing I find from my own hands wishing to buy of me—

Now these women have always been used to working out & it would be far better for them to go to work for reasonable wages & their rations—both in regard to health & in furtherance of their family wellbeing—Say their husbands get 10 to 12— or 13$ per month and out of that feed their wives and from 1 to 3 or 4 children—& clothe the family—   It is impossible for one man to do this & maintain his wife in idleness without stealing more or less of their support, whereas if their wives (where they are able) were at work for rations & fair wages—which they can all get; the family could live in some comfort & more happily—besides their labor is a very important percent of the entire labor of the South—& if not made avaible, must affect to some extent the present crop—   Now is a very important time in the crop—& the weather being good & to continue so for the remainder of the year, I think it would be a good thing to put the women to work and all that is necessary to do this in most cases is an order from you directing the agents to require the women to make contracts for the balance of the year—   I have several that are working well—while others and generally younger ones who have husbands & from 1 to 3 or 4 children are idle—indeed refuse to work & say their husbands must support them.   Now & then there is a woman who is not able to work in the field—or who has 3 or 4 children at work & can afford to live on her childrens labobor—with that of her husband—   Even in such a case it would be better she should be at work—   Generally however most of them should be in the field—

Could not this matter be referred to your agents   They are generally very clever men and would do right   I would suggest that you give this matter your favorable consideration & if you can do so to use your influence to make these idle women go to work.   You would do them & the country a service besides gaining favor & the good opinion of the people generally

I beg you will not consider this matter lightly for it is a very great evil & one that the Bureau ought to correct—if they wish the Freedmen & women to do well— I have 4 or 5 good women hands now idle that ought to be at work becase their families cannot really be supported honestly without it   This should not be so—& you will readily see how important it is to change it at once— I am very respectfully Your obt servant

M. C. Fulton

I am very willing to carry my idle women to the Bureau agency & give them such wages as the Agent may think fair—& I will further garanty that they shall be treated kindly & not over worked— I find a general complaint on this subject every where I go—and I have seen it myself and experienced its bad effects among my own hands— These idle women are bad examples to those at work & they are often mischief makers— having no employment their brain becomes more or less the Devil's work shop as is always the case with idle people—black or white & quarrels & Musses among the colored people generally can be traced to these idle folks that are neither serving God—Man or their country—

Are they not in some sort vagrants as they are living without employment—and mainly without any visible means of support—and if so are they not amenable to vagrant act—? They certainly should be— I may be in error in this matter but I have no patience with idleness or idlers   Such people are generally a nuisance—& ought to be reformed if possible or forced to work for a support— Poor white women (and such too have [. . .] & business) have to work— so should all poor people—or else stealing must be legalized—or tolerated for it is the twin sister of idleness—[24]

ALS

Former slaves' efforts to control their own domestic lives came into immediate and continuing conflict with former slaveholders' assertion of a claim to their labor. When other methods proved inadequate, self-appointed "regulator" groups—precursors to the Ku Klux Klan—roamed the countryside, threatening recalcitrant freedpeople with violence and, all too often, acting on those threats. In January 1867, the following broadside was found nailed to the door of freedpeople's houses in Robertson and Sumner counties, Tennessee; in at least one neighborhood persons claiming to have been appointed to enforce its provisions also read it aloud to the freedpeople. Heading the broadside's demands was an insistence that black women and children return to working for white employers.

I AM
COMMITTEE

1st. No man shall squat negroes on his place unless they are all under his employ male and female.

2d. Negro women shall be employed by white persons

3d. All children shall be hired out for something.

4th. Negroes found in cabins to themselves shall suffer the penalty.

5th. Negroes shall not be allowed to hire negroes.

6th. Idle men, women or children, shall suffer the penalty.

7th. All white men found with negroes in secret places shall be dealt with and those that hire negroes must pay promptly and act with good faith to the negro. I will make the negro do his part, and the white must too.

8th. For the first offence is one hundred lashes—the second is looking up a sap lin.

9th. This I do for the benefit of all young or old, high and tall, black and white. Any one that may not like these rules can try their luck, and see whether or not I will be found doing my duty.

10th. Negroes found stealing from any one or taking from their employers to other negroes, death is the first penalty.

11th. Running about late of nights shall be strictly dealt with.

12th. White man and negro, I am everywhere. I have friends in every place, do your duty and I will have but little to do.

Even when their poverty made it necessary for all family members to hire as plantation laborers, former slave families usually tried to deal with the employer as an economic unit, and husbands and fathers often felt it their responsibility to stand between the employer and their wives and children. A freedman on a Mississippi plantation asserted his authority as husband over the prerogatives of the employer, by interfering with his wife's assignment to a task he considered dangerous. The employer countered with a complaint before the local Freedmen's Bureau agent.

[*Jackson, Miss.*]   Sept. 2nd, 1867.

Name of Complainant.   S. G. Wilson, (white,)
Residence.

Name of person Charged,   Jackson Irving, (Colored)
Residence,   Gus. Henry^s plan., 7 1/2 miles from Jackson.

Charges Irving, with disobeying his Orders refusing to let his Wife assist the other Women in Weighing down the lever. to raise the Gin House,

Jacob Thompson, (Colored) Sworn, (Head of the squad,)   States that all the Women in the Squad were Working at the gin House,   Jackson came and asked me what work Was to be done after the gin house was finished, then said he would get his Wife at other Work, then told his Wife to go away when Mr Wilson told Amy, (Irvings wife) to Come back. Irving ordered her to not to obey him, saying to Wilson if you have any thing to Say I am the man to talk to,

Julia Coleman, (Colored) Sworn,   States that she was one of the Squad at Work, at the Gin, that the Work was not hard, and that she did not think she was doing any Work that did not belong to her.   Was there when Irving Sent his Wife away.   When Mr Wilson, called to Amy,

Irving told to her to go on, Saying to Mr Wilson, if you have any thing to say, Say it to me,

Jackson Irving, States in defence that he was afraid his wife might get injured, he admits that he told her to leave, and told her to go away after Mr Wilson called to her, *Decision*, Jackson Irving Acknowledged he Was Wrong before the Squad, promises not to interfere hereafter with the Work assigned his Wife, and that he will himself work steadily during the remainder of the Year. Mr Wilson expressed himself Satisfied With this Settlement,[26]

HD

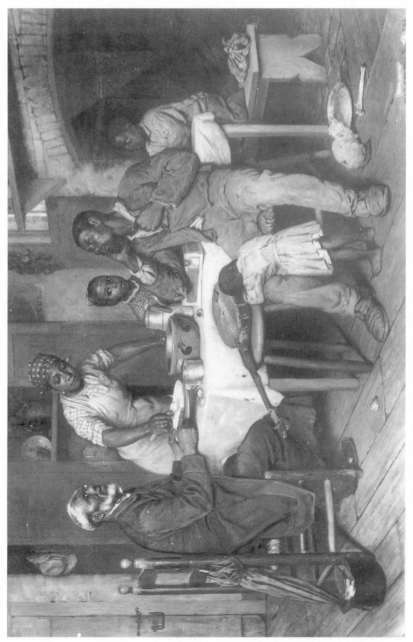

A family at fireside. (Richard Norris Brooke, *A Pastoral Visit*, Library of Congress)

CHAPTER

PARENTS AND CHILDREN

ONE OF THE SLAVES' PRINCIPAL INDICTMENTS OF chattel slavery was its violation of the bond between parent and child. Slave fathers and mothers had no legal claim to their sons and daughters, who, like themselves, were property. Parents directed the activities of their children, shaped the conditions of their daily lives, and guided their development under circumstances dictated by the owner, not the parents. Enslavement similarly constrained the ability of adult children to provide for their aging mothers and fathers. More fundamental still, slaveowners determined whether parents and children remained in contact at all, for with the spread of the cotton kingdom across the Lower South, tens of thousands of children and young adults were taken from their families and sold into the interstate slave trade.

In defiance of their owners' power, slaves affirmed the connection of parent to child, delighted in the affection that flowed between them, and defined for themselves the responsibilities each bore to the other. Finding support in a slave community that saw the rearing of children as a collective endeavor, parents prepared

their children as best they could for the travail of slavery, while
never yielding in their harsh judgment of the slaveholders who
made that preparation necessary. Slaves thus expected that freedom should mean, above all, the opportunity to gain control over
their own progeny.

The fulfillment—or frustration—of that expectation shaped the
process by which the African-American family remade itself in the
era of emancipation. Like the obligations of husband and wife,
those of parent and child generally found expression in the pat-
terns of daily life rather than in formal pronouncements. But disputes between former slaves and former owners over the custody of
children, as well as conflicts among parents themselves, brought to
the surface the unspoken standards that governed the relationships of parents and children and the emotional ties that buttressed them.

Contests over children's labor figured prominently in these disputes, for the familial bond was economic as well as emotional. The
labor of children was as essential to the support of the freedpeople's households as it was to the material enterprise and domestic
comfort of the former slaveholders. To reassert control over what
had been unquestionably theirs under slavery, former owners
employed apprenticeship laws that bound black children to unpaid
labor until they reached adulthood. In challenging such apprenticeships, freed parents recognized the economic importance of their
children to the family's survival but also asserted a fuller understanding of familial bonds.

Former slaveholders who were unwilling to relinquish control
over black children did not hesitate to jettison elderly people whose
working lives had been spent in their service. Emancipation, they
argued, had freed them of any obligation to support such unfortu-
nates. While denouncing the former owners' callous repudiation of
responsibility, freedpeople almost universally accepted—and often
welcomed—the duty of caring for aged parents. Although the burden was often a heavy one, nothing more surely confirmed their
commitment to the reciprocal obligations of parent and child.

In tones that resounded with the accumulated frustrations of generations of black parents, Spotswood Rice, a soldier from Missouri,
hurled defiance at the slaveholder's claim to his children. Drawing
strength from the Union's commitment to emancipation and his
own participation in the army of freedom, Private Rice assured
first his daughters and then the woman who owned one of them
that his rights as their father would soon prevail.

[Benton Barracks Hospital, St. Louis, Mo., September 3, 1864]
My Children   I take my pen in hand to rite you A few lines to let you
know that I have not forgot you and that I want to see you as bad as
ever   now my Dear Children I want you to be contented with whatever
may be your lots   be assured that I will have you if it cost me my life
on the 28th of the mounth. 8 hundred White and 8 hundred blacke
solders expects to start up the rivore to Glasgow and above there thats
to be jeneraled by a jeneral that will give me both of you   when they
Come I expect to be with, them and expect to get you both in
return.   Dont be uneasy my children   I expect to have you.   If Diggs
dont give you up this Government will and I feel confident that I will get
you   Your Miss Kaitty said that I tried to steal you   But I'll let her
know that god never intended for man to steal his own flesh and
blood.   If I had no cofidence in God I could have confidence in
her   But as it is If I ever had any Confidence in her I have none now
and never expect to have   And I want her to remember if she meets me
with ten thousand soldiers she [will?] meet her enemy   I once [*thought*]
that I had some respect for them but now my respects is worn out and
have no sympathy for Slaveholders.   And as for her cristianantty I
expect the Devil has Such in hell   You tell her from me that She is the
frist Christian that I ever hard say that aman could Steal his own child
especially out of human bondage

You can tell her that She can hold to you as long as she can   I never would expect to ask her again to let you come to me because I know that the devil has got her hot set againsts that that is write   now my Dear children I am a going to close my letter to you   Give my love to all enquiring friends   tell them all that we are well and want to see them very much and Corra and Mary receive the greater part of it you sefves   and dont think hard of us not sending you any thing   I you father have a plenty for you when I see you   Spott & Noah sends their love to both of you   Oh! My Dear children how I do want to see you

HL   [*Spotswood Rice*]¹

[*Benton Barracks Hospital, St. Louis, Mo., September 3, 1864*]

I received a leteter from Cariline telling me that you say I tried to steal to plunder my child away from you   now I want you to understand that mary is my Child and she is a God given rite of my own and you may hold on to hear as long as you can but I want you to remembor this one thing that the longor you keep my Child from me the longor you will have to burn in hell and the qwicer youll get their   for we are now makeing up a bout one thoughsand blacke troops to Come up tharough and wont to come through Glasgow and when we come wo be to Copperhood rabbels and to the Slaveholding rebbels for we dont expect to leave them there root neor branch   but we thinke how ever that we that have Children in the hands of you devels we will trie your [vertues?] the day that we enter Glasgow   I want you to understand kittey diggs that where ever you and I meets we are enmays to each orthere   I offered once to pay you forty dollers for my own Child but I am glad now that you did not accept it   Just hold on now as long as you can and the worse it will be for you   you never in you life befor I came down hear did you give Children any thing not eny thing whatever

not even a dollers worth of expencs   now you call my children your
pro[*per*]ty   not so with me   my Children is my own and I expect to
get them and when I get ready to come after mary I will have bout a
powrer and autherity to bring hear away and to exacute vengencens on
them that holds my Child   you will then know how to talke to me   I
will assure that and you will know how to talk rite too   I want you now
to just hold on to hear if you want to   iff your conchosence tells thats
the road go that road and what it will brig you to kittey diggs   I have
no fears about geting mary out of your hands   this whole Government
gives chear to me and you cannot help your self

ALS   Spotswood Rice[2]

> Another soldier unsuccessfully sought a discharge so that he could
> provide for the needs of his wife and children, whose owner would
> not maintain them.

Taylors Barrecks [*Louisville, Ky.*]   December 4th 1864
Mr Abrham Lincoln   I have one recest to make to you that is I ask you
to dis Charge me for I have a wife and she has four Children   thay
have a hard master one that loves the South hangs with it   he dos not
giv them a rage [*rag*] nor havnot for too yars   I have found* all   he
says let old Abe Giv them Close   if I had them I raise them up but I am
here and if you will free me and hir and heir Children with me I Can
take Cair of them

She lives with David Sparks in Oldham Co Ky

My Woman is named Malindia Jann my daughter Adline Clyte and

---

*I.e., provided.

Women and children near Alexandria, Virginia. (private collection, courtesy of Michael Musick)

Malindia Eler and Cleman Tine and Natthanel Washington and my
name is George Washington   heir in Taylors Barrecks and my famaly
suferring   I have sent forty dollars worth to them cence I have bin heir
and that is all I have and I have not drawn any thing cence I have bin
heir   I am forty eight years   my woman thirty three   I ask this to
your oner to a blige yours &c   your un Grateful Servent

ALS   George Washington[3]

> The enlistment of black soldiers did not always entail separation
> from their families. In Union-occupied parts of the Confederacy,
> parents, wives, and children often lived in contraband camps near
> the soldiers' bivouacs, enjoying a measure of security by virtue of
> these arrangements. But in the slave states that had remained in
> the Union, federal commanders refused sanctuary to the soldiers'
> families, even going so far as to expel them from army encamp-
> ments. Joseph Miller, a soldier from Kentucky, described the heart-
> less treatment of his wife and children, and his melancholy dis-
> charge of a father's final duty.

Camp Nelson Ky   November 26, 1864

Personally appered before me E. B W Restieaux Capt. and Asst.
Quartermaster Joseph Miller a man of color who being duly sworn upon
oath says

I was a slave of George Miller of Lincoln County Ky.   I have always
resided in Kentucky and am now a Soldier in the service of the United
States.   I belong to Company I 124 U. S. C[*olored*]. Inft now Stationed
at Camp Nelson Ky.   When I came to Camp for the purpose of enlisting
about the middle of October 1864 my wife and children came with me
because my master said that if I enlisted he would not maintain them
and I knew they would be abused by him when I left.   I had then four

children ages respectively ten nine seven and four years.   On my presenting myself as a recruit I was told by the Lieut. in command to take my family into a tent within the limits of the Camp.   My wife and family occupied this tent by the express permission of the aforementioned Officer and never received any notice to leave until Tuesday November 22" when a mounted guard gave my wife notice that she and her children must leave Camp before early morning.   This was about six O'clock at night.   My little boy about seven years of age had been very sick and was slowly recovering   My wife had no place to go and so remained until morning.   About eight Oclock Wednesday morning November 23" a mounted guard came to my tent and ordered my wife and children out of Camp   The morning was bitter cold.   It was freezing hard.   I was certain that it would kill my sick child to take him out in the cold.   I told the man in charge of the guard that it would be the death of my boy   I told him that my wife and children had no place to go and I told him that I was a soldier of the United States.   He told me that it did not make any difference.   he had orders to take all out of Camp.   He told my wife and family that if they did not get up into the wagon which he had he would shoot the last one of them.   On being thus threatened my wife and children went into the wagon   My wife carried her sick child in her arms.   When they left the tent the wind was blowing hard and cold and having had to leave much of our clothing when we left our master, my wife with her little one was poorly clad.   I followed them as far as the lines.   I had no Knowledge where they were taking them.   At night I went in search of my family.   I found them at Nicholasville about six miles from Camp.   They were in an old meeting house belonging to the colored people.   The building was very cold having only one fire.   My wife and children could not get near the fire, because of the number of colored people huddled together by the soldiers. I found my wife and children shivering with cold and famished with hunger They had not recieved a morsel of food during the whole day. My boy was dead. He died directly after getting down from the wagon. I Know he was Killed by exposure to the inclement weather I had to return to camp that night so I left my family in the meeting house and walked back. I had walked there. I travelled in all twelve miles Next morning I walked to Nicholasville. I dug a grave myself and buried my own child. I left my family in the Meeting house—where they still remain And further this deponent saith not

his

HDeSr   (Signed) Joseph   Miller[4]

mark

The northern press published the affidavits of Joseph Miller and others who had witnessed the expulsion, and the resulting furor— together with protests through military channels—resulted in the establishment at Camp Nelson of a "refugee home" for black soldiers' families.[5]

Distance did not obliterate the responsibilities of parenthood. Harrison Smith, a Kentucky soldier stationed in faraway Texas, felt nonetheless entitled to make decisions regarding the welfare of his son. When sickness prevented the boy's mother from caring for him, Smith's sister-in-law took him in. But the mother had no intention of yielding permanent custody, and conflict ensued between the two women, especially after the mother began living with another man. Informed of his wife's infidelity, Harrison Smith instructed his sister-in-law to take the boy. Seeking authority from the Freedmen's Bureau to do so, she swore the following affidavit and placed in evidence a letter she had received from the child's father.

Louisville, Ky.   April 3ᵈ *1867*

Minta Smith colored being sworn says that she is married to a man
named Alexander Smith and lives in the city of Louisville.   That her
husband's Brother Harrison Smith enlisted in the Army some time in
March or first of April 1865   That Harrison Smith had one child a boy
now about seven years old.   That some time about the first of December
1865 she asked the mother's permission to take the child to her house
for a while and she agreed to it

That a short time afterwards the mother was taken down with the
small Pox and by the authorities was sent to the Pest house and was
there about one month.   That after getting from the Pest house she (the
mother) frequently came to the house of this affiant to see her and to see
the child and once during the first of this year she asked that the boy be
returned to her.   This affiant said to her she was not able to take care of
the boy and as the Father had several times expressed the wish that the
boy should remain with her she hoped that it would be done.   That
during the last high water the houses in the neighborhood where they
were living were all overflowed and the most of the tenants had to
remove to other houses and during the time of removal from the overflow
the mother again got possession of the boy and will not let her the affiant
have him again

That about ten months since the mother of the boy commenced living
with a man by the name of James Downs colored and that for the last
four months they have kept house and lived together as man and wife
without being married

That Harrison Smith sent his wife the mother of the boy money at
different times until he heard that she had taken up with and was living
with the man Downs and that soon after he heard that he wrote to this

affiant to take his boy and take care of him until he the Father came
home   This last letter is dated at Fort Bliss Texas   March 9 /67 and is
herewith filed

her

Minta ✕ Smith[6]

mark

HDSr

[*Enclosure*]   fort bliss   texas   March th 9 1867
My dear sister   I write you this letter to let you no I am well   Mintey
I ask of you in this letter to go and take my boy from my wilf as sh is not
doeing write by him   take him and keep him untill I com home   if sh
is not willing to gave him up go to the fried mands bury [*Freedmen's
Bureau*] and shoe this letter   it is my recust for you to have him   I
doe not want her to have my child with an another man   she is not
living writ to rase children   I feel for my child becase I no I have agod
mother   I would lik for my child to be rased well   take god cear of
him   I will be hom next fall if I live   asholder stand abad chanc but if
god spars me I will be home   I have nothing more to say but I still
remain your true brother

Harison smith

write soon[7]

ALS

> But Harrison Smith was not alone in asserting a parental claim.
> Harriet Ann Bridwell, the boy's mother, defended—by reason of
> economic necessity—her decision to accept the protection of
> another man and protested against the delivery of her son to any-
> one but his father.

Louisville, Ky.   April 3^{d} 1867

Harriet Ann Bridwell colored being sworn says that some eight years since she married Harrison Smith

That they were married according to the usages and customs among slaves.   That by him she had two children one of which is dead and the other now over seven years of age and the one in controversy between Minta Smith and herself   That after her husband Harrison Smith enlisted in the army she could not keep up and support herself and her child and she under these circumstances was induced to accept the offers of protection made her by James Bridwell sometimes called Downes and she is now living with and keeping his house as his wife although they have not been married by license obtained from the proper authority

She further says she is willing to Deliver the child to his Father but she does not want others to have him before the Father comes home   She says that she asked Minta Smith more than once for the child and Minty would answer her that she (meaning me) was not able to take care of the child and to let her [*keep*] him until the Father came home

her

Harriet Ann ✕ Bridwell[8]

mark

HDSr

Labeling Bridwell "a prostitute," Freedmen's Bureau authorities ruled that the child should be delivered to Minta Smith "before its ruin is complete."[9] Harrison Smith himself was evidently not so quick to judge his former wife wholly unfit to rear their son. A few weeks after the bureau ordered the boy removed from her custody, Harriet Ann Bridwell appeared at bureau headquarters bearing new instructions from the father.

[*Louisville, Ky.*]   May 28 [*1867*]

In The case of Minta Smith colored against the mother of the child of Hamilton Smith now in the army and stationed at EL. Passo Texas. on the 8" of last month the child was awarded to Minta under the instructions of the Father in a letter exhibited by her.   To day the mother comes and exhibits letters from the Father which are properly Post marked and in which he says he wants the mother to have the possession of the child and the child at the present being with the mother she is permitted to keep it untill further advised[10]

HD

The obligations of parents and children were reciprocal, with responsibility for emotional and material support shifting to the children as parents aged and themselves became dependent. Apprehensive about her son's safety as well as her own survival, the elderly mother of a black soldier from Pennsylvania petitioned Abraham Lincoln for his release from further service, on the grounds that he was her sole support.

Carlisles [*Pa.*]   nov 21 1864

Mr abarham lincon   I wont to knw sir if you please wether I can have my son relest from the arme   he is all the subport I have now   his father is Dead and his brother that wase all the help that I had   he has bean wonded twise   he has not had nothing to send me yet   now I am old and my head is blossaming for the grave and if you dou I hope the lord will bless you and me   if you please answer as soon as you can if you please   tha say that you will simpethise withe the poor   thear wase awhite jentel man told me to write to you   Mrs jane Welcom if you please answer it to

he be long to the eight rigmat co a u st colard troops   mart welcom is his name   he is a sarjent

AL   [*Jane Welcome*][11]

President Lincoln forwarded Jane Welcome's letter to the Bureau of Colored Troops, which informed her that "the interests of the service will not permit that your request be granted."[12]

———•———

A nineteen-year-old soldier from Schoharie County, New York, who had not seen his widowed mother for two years, applied for a furlough after the deaths of his siblings left her without anyone to make preparations for the coming winter. He addressed his request to an unidentified official.

U S Genar hospital   fort monroe VA hampton VA   Sptember th 26th 1865
My kind friend   i Take my pen in hand to Let yoo know that i am not
Well at present but I hop that these few Lines may find you the
Same   I Want to ask yoo a few questions if you Will allow me to   if
yoo Wont yoo please to Let me go home alittle While   I Want to go
home for a While to stay for my mothr is Sike and Would Lieke go hom
on furlough for 30 deys   I Want to go home Very much to see my
[*mother*]   if you please Let me go home   my mothr is sicke for I have
not seen her for tow years   my mothr is old and Lik to go and he for
While   I have maid aplication for furlough on the fifth of Sptember
and it has not Come yet for the doctor of my Ward singed my aplication
but they dont Care for us her in the hospital   i want to get home once
more to See my poor old mothr   my mothr is fifty 3 years old and She
is hall i have got   my mother Lives in poor Shanty and has not any one
to get Wood for her next winter   i wish that you let me have a furlough
for 30 days if you please to Grant me my furlough I Cant thank you
anough for my [*mother*] has not seen my face for two years   i think it
iS high time that try and go and see her   please to write and let me

Schoolboys in South Carolina. (Photographs and Prints Division, Schomburg Center for Research in Black Culture, New York Public Library, Astor, Lenox and Tilden Foundations)

know if please thy Wont make out a furlough   my mother is Sik and
the family is all diying off   if i Stay much longer I Will not See any of
my folks to home   My mother lost all her Children this fall Whill I Was
in the Serveice U. S.   thy can have all my money if they want it if they
for I did not Comme out for the money for I Was a fraid of geting
drafted and I thought that Would enlist   When that order was given
out for to muster out all in the hospital I Was put down for muster out
and thy have not Let me go yet   the doctors ar very mean   they Wont
give us our discharge at all

My father is dead   My mother farther is deaed   my mothr is
Widow and So here left alone for Ever   Yours respctfully obedient
Servent

ALS   Richard Henry Tebout[13]

Tebout, who had been wounded at the battle of Petersburg, was
ordered to report to New York for muster out of service.[14]

Parents whose sons marched off to war feared more than the loss of
their material support. A military comrade penned the following
letter of consolation to the bereaved mother of Corporal William
Guy, a soldier from Maryland who had died in combat.

Near Petersburge [*Va.*]   August 19th 1864
Dear Madam   I receave A letter from You A few day Ago inquir in
regard to the Fait of Your Son   I am sarry to have to inform You that
thear is no dobt of his Death   he Died A Brave Death in Trying to
Save the Colors of Rige[*ment*] in that Dreadful Battil   Billys Death

was unevesally [*mourned*] by all but by non greatter then by my
self   ever sins we have bin in the Army we have bin amoung the moust
intimoat Friend   wen every our Rige[*ment*] wen into Camp he sertan
to be at my Tent and meney happy moment we seen to gether Talking
about Home and the Probability of our Living to get Home to See each
other Family and Friend   But Providence has will other wise and You
must Bow to His will   You and His Wife Sister and all Have my
deepust Simppathy and trust will be well all in this Trying moment

You Inquired about Mr Young   He wen to the Hospetol and I can
not give You eney other information in regard to Him

Billys thing that You requested to inquired about I can git no informa
of as in the bustil of the Battil every thing was Lost

Give my Respects to Samual Jackson and Family not forgeting Your
self and Family   I remain Your Friend

ALS   G. H. Freeman[15]

> News of a child's death came as a heavy blow. Martha Wells, the
> mother of a West Virginia soldier, clung to the hope that a mistake
> had been made, that identities had been confused, that her son was
> still alive. She asked the adjutant general's office to reexamine the
> records.

Berkeley Springs   Morgan County   W. V^a.   Decr 24th 1866.
Dr Sir   I received your very prompt reply to my letter of the 6th Nov^r
/66. making inquiry about my son Gus: Wells of C°. I.—38 Regimt US
Troops of Volunteers, and your answer to me is that Gus: Wells Died in
Hospital at Brownsville Texas. during the month of October 1865.   Now
my dear Sir as a fond mother I am still in doubt about his death
thinking that it might be another Gus: Wells that has died: as there is a

colored soldier here who says he left him well at Brownsville after that date and he has lead me to believe what he tells me is the truth   I therefore have concluded that there might be another of the same name *dead* and not my *son*:   if it is a mistake I know you can find it out and let me know— I hope you will make the search and gratify a poor distressed mother.   it will give me satisfaction to know his color his age his height, &c which I suppose his officers have down on their Books and if I am Satisfied in my distressed mind that my son is dead I will go to Texas & Bring him Home: I hope you will give me the name of the Hospital Doctor. and let me know if I can get him   please let me know the distance to Texas and what it would cost   now dear Sir I hope you will not consider me putting you to too much trouble in making these inquiries about my son when you consider that I am a fond mother and now a distressed mother being in doubts about the death of my son   as I have said there may be *one* of the same name in the same Regement who has *died* at that time   if so you can soon find out and let me know.   the Doctor of the Hospital I suppose can give full information I will be under many obligations for any further information from you and this will relieve a fond but distressed mothers mind   please tell me know if he died with a wound or natural sickness   I am your Humble and obedient Servant

Martha Wells

in great Haste.[16]

ALS

[*Endorsement*]   Augustus Wells, Pvt. Co "I" 38 U.S.C.I. Died at Post Hospl. Brownsville Texas. October 2[d] 1865.   Chronic Diarrhoea

Formal emancipation came to Maryland on November 1, 1864, months before the end of the Civil War. But the new state constitution had no sooner taken effect than former slaveholders inaugurated a campaign to circumscribe the ex-slaves' liberty and undermine the integrity of their families. Over the protests of newly freed mothers and fathers, hundreds of former owners availed themselves of the antebellum apprenticeship laws to have black children bound to them. A federal military officer on Maryland's Eastern Shore found himself beseiged by frantic parents who feared the loss of freedom's promise: a secure family.

Easton [*Md.*], November 4th 1864

General:— There is a persistant determination of the disloyal people of this County, to totally disregard the laws of Maryland, in regard to Slavery.   Immediately after the Governer issued his Proclamation, declaring the New Constitution adopted, a rush was made to the Orphan's Court of this County, for the purpose of having all children under twenty one years of age, bound to their former owners, under the apprentice law of the State.   In many instances, boys of 12 and 14 years are taken from their parents, under the pretence that they (the parents) are incapable of supporting them, while the younger children are left to be maintained by the parents.   This is done without obtaining the parent's consent, and in direct violation of the provisions of the Act of Assembly, and almost in every instance by disloyal parties.   Two of the members of the Orphan's Court being bitter enemies of the present organic law of the state, seem to be so prejudiced agains these poor creatures, that they do not regard their rights.   The Court, as yet, has never taken any testimony relative to the capability of the parents to support their children, and where the parents are willing to bind them,

TO WHOM IT MAY CONCERN!

Warning is hereby given that the undersigned has arrived in these counties with orders to *BREAK UP* the practice now prevalent of

Apprenticing Negroes

without the consent of their parents, to their former masters or others. And if necessary to arrest all persons, who refuse liberty to such apprentices, or withold them from their parents, and keep them in custody until they consent to such liberation. Also to offer to all such parents as may not be able to maintain their children a free passage to the *"Freedman's Home"* in Baltimore if so desired.

The undersigned will be in the several Eastern Shore Counties for some time and may be addressed at Cambridge, Md., where for the present he has established his Head-quarters.

HENRY H. LOCKWOOD.

Brigadier General.

Dec. 6, 1864.

Circular posted on Maryland's Eastern Shore by a Union general. (National Archives) they have been denied the choice of homes. In plain terms—the Rebels here are showing an evident determination to still hold this people in bondage, and call upon the Orphan's Court to give their proceeding the sanction of law.

My office is visited every day by numbers of these poor creatures, asking for redress, which I have not the power to give. They protest before the Court against binding their children to their former masters, who have dubtless treated them cruelly, and yet that same Court declares them vagrants, before they have enjoy liberty a single week.— in many instances before they have ever been permitted to leave their masters. The law in all instances requires the child or the parents' consent, but it is not done by Talbot County law. I am fearful there will be trouble here if measures are not taken to stop the proceeding. Loyalty is outraged, and justice has become a mockery.

I can furnish you with the names of the parties,—aggrieving and aggrieved—but am merly writing now, to inform you of the state of affairs existing here. Had I authority in the premises, I would stop the proceeding: Or did I occupy the position of a military command, I should lay an injunction on the Court until I could hear from you. But as it is, I can only warn you of impending danger.

Hoping you will receive this in kindness, and believe me actuated by patriotic motives in writing it, I remain Respectfully Your Obedient Servant

HLS   Andrew Stafford[17]

When Jane Kamper learned that her former master regarded her children's apprenticeship as the price of her freedom, she took their recovery into her own hands.

Bal^{to} [*Md.*] Novr 14" /64

Statement of Jane Kamper

Slave of Wm Townsend of Talbot County Md.

I was the slave of Wm Townsend of Talbot county & told Mr. Townsend of my having become free & desired my master to give my children & my bedclothes   he told me that I was free but that my Children Should be bound to me [*him*].   he locked my Children up so that I could not find them   I afterwards got my children by stealth & brought them to Baltimore.   I desire to regain possession of my bed clothes & furniture.

My Master pursued me to the Boat to get possession of my children but I hid them on the boat

her

Jane ✕ Kamper (f[*ree*] n[*egro*])[18]

mark

HDSr

The sale of slaves and the ownership of family members by different masters had so fragmented many slave families that the task of
reuniting them after emancipation seemed nearly hopeless. When
Milly Johnson, a freedwoman in North Carolina, set out to locate
the five children who had been taken from her, she could provide the
Freedmen's Bureau with reliable information about the location of
only one of them.

Chapel Hill, N.C.   March, 26th 1867.

Sir:—. . . .

It is my purpose, to advertise for my children,

When I last knew them they were 2 of them in Esics county V^a a girl and Boy, Living with their former owners.   The Boy Belonged to Hugh Billaps   The Girl Belonged to Dr Richards.   The Boys name was Musco Johnson—   The Girl Letty Johnson   This accounts for 2—

There is another two a Girl and Boy.   They were sold to speculators
at Richmond V^a Where they were carried I do not Know.   the girl's
name was Henrietta Johnson   The Boy William Quals Johnson.
There is still another Anna Johnson who is Living in Hertford Co., N.C.
with Mr. Albert Elliott my former owner and since the [*Confederate*]
surrender he took her from me   I protested against but of no avail   I
have tried several times since to get her.   I wrote to him Last year and
he would make no reply to my letters.   he said when he took my child
that she belonged to him, and I herd that his wife said that she intended
to Keep her till she was 21 years of age.   all this was done against my
will.   Now Sir I want her.   if I cannot hear from the others she can be
gotten I presume

Now Sir:

You will do me a lasting favor to attend to this matter for me as
promptly as possible   I convey the Matter into your hands,—hopeing
that there can some information be gained from my children

Intrusting the matter with you sir I am Very Resptfully Sir:—

HLSr   Milly Johnson[19]

> The Freedmen's Bureau succeeded in restoring Anna to her
> mother, and bureau agents in Virginia and North Carolina eventu-
> ally produced information regarding the possible whereabouts of
> both Letty and Musco. But clues about the fate of Henrietta and
> William Quals had burned with the slave traders' records.

—•—

> Throughout the South, former slaveowners searched for ways to
> retain control over the lives and labor of their erstwhile slaves.
> Among their most effective techniques was manipulating the ex-
> slaves' family ties. Two years after the general emancipation, an

Georgia

Washington County } Before me came
Rebecca Parsons - A freedwoman of
this County who being duly sworn de
poseth & Saith, that She was when freed
by the Government a Slave of J A Parsons of Johnson County - That She
has four Children now in Possession
of Said Parsons - That when she
was freed She informed Said Parsons that She was going to her Kin
dred who lived in Elbert County
Ga - He told her that she might go
but her Children belonged to Him
& She Should not have them - That
She was thus compelled to remain
with Him - That in September last
because she had hired one of the Children
to work with a neighbor and refused
to take her and place her with Him
Said Parsons Cruelly beat her deponent
and drove her from his place

thus separating her from her children
That she found a home in Washington County & in February last she went to Parsons & demanded her children — That Parsons told her "they were bound to him and that she should not have them unless she paid him four thousand dollars" That she was thus compelled to return without them — And she left them crying to go with her

Sworn to and   her
Subscribed before me   Rebecca X Parsons
this 28th April 1867   mark

James R Smith Agent
Bureau. F. R & A L for
Washington County

agent of the Freedmen's Bureau recorded the affidavit of Rebecca
Parsons, a freedwoman whose children yet remained in the hands
of their old master. By refusing to release the children, the former
owner had retained not only their labor but also that of their
mother, who would not leave without them. When she renewed her
efforts to claim them, he resorted to means of domination drawn
from both the familiar repertoire of slavery and the new conditions
of freedom: he punished her with personal violence and formalized
his control over the children by having them bound to him under
the state apprenticeship laws.

Georgia   Washington County   28th April 1867

Before me came Rebecca Parsons—a freedwoman of this County who
being duly sworn deposeth & saith, that she was when freed by the
Government a Slave of T A Parsons of Johnson County—   That she has
four children now in possession of said Parsons—   That when she was
freed she informed said Parsons that she was going to her kindred who
lived in Elbert County Ga—   He told her that she might go but her
children belonged to Him & she should not have them—   That she was
thus compelled to remain with Him—   That in September last because
she had hired one of the children to work with a neighbor and refused to
take her and place her with Him said Parsons cruelly beat her deponent
and drove her from his place thus separating her from her children

That she found a home in Washington County & in February last she
went to Parsons & demanded her children—   That Parsons told her
"they were bound to him and that she should not have them unless she
paid Him four thousand dollars"   That she was thus compelled to
return without them—And she left them crying to go with Her

her

Rebecca ✕ Parsons[20]

mark

HDSr

Former slaves and their children. (*Harper's Weekly,* Mar. 24, 1863)

The freedpeople's struggle to constitute their families as economic
units with authority over the allocation of their own labor con-
flicted directly with the determination of planters and other former
slaveowners to command the labor of the former slaves. In many
parts of the South, especially in the first years of freedom, the labor
of teenage children became a particular object of contention. In the
hands of the planters and compliant civil officials, state apprenticeship laws, which ostensibly provided for orphans and for children
whose parents could not support them, became a means of compelling the labor of children old enough to work as full field hands.
A master gained the uncompensated labor of an apprentice until he
or she reached adulthood—an interval easily lengthened by falsify-
ing the age of the child at the time of the legal binding. Moreover,
by seizing older children while leaving younger nonworkers to be
supported by their parents, the planters undermined the economic
independence of ex-slave families like that of Enoch Braston. Braston's affidavit is preceded by the report of an army chaplain who
was serving as a Freedmen's Bureau agent.

Grenada [*Miss.*]   Jan 10" 1866

Col.   I have the honor to report the inclosed affidavits of freedmen, as
samples of general cases.   My office is & has been crowded from "early
morn to dewey eve" with complaints similar to these.   There is "none to
plead the cause of the poor."   I am yet to know the first case where a
negro has carried his cause to the civil officers & a suit in his behalf
commenced, & much less justice done him by way of council or getting a
settlement.

I state what from my observation seems the fact "there is no law for
the darkie, that a white man is bound to respect."   I have written quires
of paper & sent scores of Tho's Circular No 9* & it amounts to just
about as one of the darkis said when he came back, "Now Probo Maser

*Issued on August 4, 1865, by Colonel Samuel Thomas,
Freedmen's Bureau assistant commissioner for the state of
Mississippi, Circular 9 denounced at length the widespread

[*provost marshal*], yus wans to git us justice, but your writins to dese
peles, help us jus as much as ifs you say to us up on house top, you's got
wings & yo can fly.   Wese trys it & wese come *flat down*!!

And it is just so!   I could send you hundreds of affidavits but such has
been the crowd around the office, this cold morning is the first
opportunity I could command to write.   Children are almost invariably
bound out from two to 12 years younger than they are.   Bosworth, the
white man that hired Braston & released him, told me he saw the papers
over Sam who is 18 years old & sam is bound out 6 years & six moths old!

I have hired out to othe partis many young persons from 12 years old
to 19 who have been apprenticed as paupers, & where a white ma[n']s
interest comes in & will stand up for the darkie, none try the strength of
their missconstrued apprentice law!!

The avaricious Slaveholder of former days, in this apprentice law, sees
a chance to effectively apply it in case of young bright & active children,
& stay not for the law to be carried out by proper officers, but run before
they are sent, snatching all irrespective of "orphanage, willingness or
ability of parents or relatives to take care of their children.   In many
cases the aged parent & gradnd parents last dependance for support is
taken away from them an in no instance has the negroes consent been
willingly obtained, but in several instances they have said "I consented
for I was afraid of my life if I did not.

.   .   .   .

ALS   L. S. Livermore[21]

physical abuse of former slaves and called on "the Planters of
Mississippi [to] both understand the new relation which they
sustain to the . . . labor of the State, and cheerfully accept the
facts of the new situation." Bureau agents were instructed to
furnish "every white Citizen in their District" with a copy of the
circular. (Vol. 31, pp. 262–66, ser. 2055, General Orders &
Circulars Issued, MS Asst. Commissioner, BRFAL [A-10892].)

[*Enclosure*]   Grenada [*Miss.*]   Jan. 10" 1866
Affidvit of Enoch Braston (colored)

I was the slave of John Heath for twelve years.   I staid with him until about the 20 of July [*1865*].   The crops were made & I had got half of the fodder pulled of which we all (fellow servnts were to have a third.   This was all he had offered us in any of the crops.

My child had the flux, & I told him I had better go to Grenada, to get medicine for it, of the Yankie doctor.   John Heath said I was getting mighty high up, & if I wanted to shew my freedom, I must get out of that yard, I could shew it there.   Said never to put another track in that yard, if I did he would put a ball through me.   I then left.

I went back at Christmas for my wife & famely.   I had hired out, to John Bosworth & family for one third of the cotton raised & half of every thing else.   I was to furnish myself—he to furnish all working utensils. Befor Christmas while I was at work with Whitticar, I went to Heaths & he offered me half I would make this year.   But I told him no.   I never could please him, so I thought we had better be apart.   He said he could not make a bargain with me   somebody had been talking with me.

I raised 13 1/2 bushels potatoes.   He sold them for six bits pr bushel & refuses to let me have any of it.

Heath refuses to pay me a dime & says he will not.

He has given a shoat to others but will not let Enoch have his pig.

At christmas day I went after my family at Heaths to begin my years worth Bosworth.

Heath said I could have Enoch 12 years old Mary 8. Silas 14 month & Peter six years old—

Graves a citizen as far as I know, was then making out the papers to bind Sam 18 years old Bob, 15 years, Hayword 13, Enoch 12 years old and Delia 10 leaving me all the youngest.   Heath said the Buzzard would pick me.   I made no reply.

I got my wife and four children.   Sam the oldest ran awy from
Heaths, while Heath was at Carolton to get his papers approved and
Sam is now with me.   After we went to Bosworths to begin our years
work, Heath & Dr Bartlet came to Bosworths (6 miles) & Said Sam
must be sent home that night, and if he did not come it would be wors
for him for he would get officers & come after him.

Bosworth advised me to leave him for Heath would bushwhack me
sometime.   I did so & brought a note to Chaplain Livermore from
Bosworth.   I then hired out to Mr Towne for $225. & all the family clear
of all expense.   My Bedding for the children and their clothing, & Bob,
15, Haywood 13, Delia 10 are all at Heaths & I dare not go after them,
for when Heath (at christmas) said buzzards would pick my bones,
Fanny Guy his stepdaughter had a doubled barrelled gun & said she
would shoot me if I came in the yard.[22]

HD

> For the impoverished former slaves—freed without land, without
> draft animals or tools, and often with few personal possessions—
> any bid for economic independence required the full commitment of
> their primary resource, the labor of their families. When Joe
> Bright, who had been free before the Civil War, and his wife and
> children, formerly slaves in Sampson County, North Carolina,
> avoided wage labor and instead rented land in neighboring Duplin
> County, their former master and other local whites attacked their
> independence by seizing the working-age children and thus wreck-
> ing their family economy.

Duplin Co [*N.C.*]   Aprl 26 1866

Worthy Cornell   I, Joe Bright col man engaged or leased 40. *Acres* of
land from Mr Joe Beason in Duplin Co NC to cultivate 2/3 off the crup
and both partnes ar Satisfied witt this arengement

from ten Children witch i have 6 to attend with me the farm and need them all to do Said labor   Also I am a mason and Plaster and can bring plenty of wittness that i am prefectly eable to Suport my family by my hard labor n work and would do right well if paple in Sampson Co would not interfear with my family matters but thay broak me down three times by taken away my help on the farm (my Children) So that I am not eable to do the work on Said farm acording my promis to *M*ʳ *Beson*   all theas Children is growing and of much use for me   the youngest of the Croud is. 12 years old the other betwen 12 and 18 years and as mutch as I know the law do not alow to bind any Childen of a freed men whare the parents is eable to Support them or thay ar over 14 years old thay can make thare one Support as this is the case hear   but still Ashaill Mathees John. Barden and frank Caroll thought thay had a better right of my Children than I had and took them from the corn feild and plow and *carried* them off to thair house   I have a trial before Mager Forster and he give me order to Keep and I took my Children but now it Seemes he take the wite mans part and alow them to Carry them off and bound them out   Is this justice?

You will oblige me very mutch to give me justis in case iff you pleas   I have no confidence in the Mager at all the way he don with me and iff I can not justes I will apeal as long as I can   Yours very respefull obeediend Servind

ALS   Joe Bright[23]

CHAPTER

VIII.

EXTENDED KINSHIP:
THE FAMILY WRIT LARGE

HE AFRICAN-AMERICAN FAMILY, AS IT EVOLVED in slavery, construed kinship in the broadest terms. Rather than look inward and shower affection on spouses and children to the exclusion of others, slaves generally looked outward and incorporated kin—grandparents, aunts and uncles, and cousins—into their understanding of family. The line between household and community was permeable and open, encompassing not only relationships by birth and marriage but also various fictive kin who became honorary "aunts" and "uncles," "brothers" and "sisters." Slaves considered all such kin, whether honorary or blood members of the family, to be "their people," and the slaves' ethos gave them special responsibility for their people. That responsibility, born of the frequent separation of parents and children, husbands and wives during slave times, continued to inform African-American family life during the Civil War and after.

Letter from Annie Davis to President Abraham Lincoln. (See p. 227)

The abolition of slavery offered black men and women the opportunity to rejoin their kin. Slaves were not allowed to travel, even to visit a spouse, children, or parents on a nearby estate, unless they had special permission from their owner. Although slaves frequently violated the strictures against travel, they did so at great risk to themselves and those on whom they called, for slaveholders, eager to maintain sovereignty over their estates, punished violators severely. Thus, although they might reside within a thicket of relatives, slaves frequently found the most elementary domestic sociability denied to them. High on the list of priorities of a Maryland woman, trying to clarify her status in the nether world of border-state emancipation, was the opportunity to visit her "people." She wrote directly to the president of the United States to ask whether she enjoyed a right fundamental to her understanding of freedom.

Belair [*Md.*]   Aug 25th 1864

Mr president   It is my Desire to be free. to go to see my people on the eastern shore.   my mistress wont let me   you will please let me know if we are free. and what i can do.   I write to you for advice.   please send me word this week. or as soon as possible and oblidge.

ALS   Annie Davis[1]

While some former slaves could reconstruct their family life with the simple act of a visit, for others the task was much more difficult. To satisfy their own material needs and aspirations, slaveholders had dealt slaves across the South like so many cards in a deck, severing established family ties and forcing slaves to spin their web of kinship anew. But forced separation did not lessen the obligations of kinship. An uncle who had been sold away from Kentucky before the birth of his three nephews hastened to his old home when he learned that their father—his brother—had died, leaving the boys without parents and apprenticed to their former master.

Louisville [*Ky.*]   November 11" 1867

Adam Woods (colored) being sworn says that his brother Pleasent Woods enlisted in the Union Army in 1864 and died while still on duty— That when Pleasent enlisted he had three children named Milton about fourteen years old. John about ten years old and Pleasant about eight years then the slaves and in the possession of Franklin Ditto in Mead County Ky

That the mother of these children was also the slave of Mr Ditto but had died before Pleasant enlisted

That in 1850 he adam was sold from Kentucky to Missouri and finally settled in Leavenworth Kansas and now makes that his home

That wanting to hear from his relations he wrote a letter to a Friend in Ky and the answer to which gave him the information of the death of his brother which answer he received about the middle of last month

That he immediately made arrangements and came to Kentucky to see about the children of his brother—

He called to see Mr Ditto and asked Mr Ditto for the children and was answered that he could not get them unless he had a legal right to them

He says that Mr Ditto Knows him well and Knows that he is the Brother of Pleasant

He says he has Four sisters living and they are all doing well.   Two of them are in this City and one in the County nearby and the other at the mouth of Salt River in Hardin County   He has also two Brothers one in this City and one at the mouth of Salt River and are doing well and each and all of them are able and willing to assist in raising and educating these children

He Further represents that he is married and has an industrious wife and a good manager, and that he owns two houses and lots in Leavenworth and has no children and is well able to raise and educate

Five generations of a family on the William Joyner Smith plantation, Beaufort, South Carolina. (Library of Congress)

the children of his deceased Brother, and his wish is to get possession of them and take them to his home in Kansas

his

Adam $\times$ Woods[2]

mark

> The bonds of kinship that Adam Woods extended to nephews he had never known encompassed relations even more distant. A freedman in Florida took special cognizance of the difficulties confronting his cousin in Montgomery, Alabama, as she struggled to support three children.

Milton Fla   June the 18th 1867.

Dear Cousin   I received word last week that you wer not doing very well in Montgomery and that times there wer very hard there   Now Sarah if you will come down here to me I will take care of you and your children and you and children shall never want for any thing as long as I have any thing to help you with   Come down and I will have a place for you and your three children for I Know that it is hard enough for a woman to get along that has a husband to help her and one that has not I do not Know how they do to get living these times   Cousin I want you to be shure and come down if you posibly can and stay here as long as you want to   if it is three or four year it will not make a bit of differance to me   Sarah you must excuse this paper and ill writen letter and bad composition for I am in a great hurry and have not much time to write for I have to go to away   But I shall look for you down here   Please come down and make your home here with my famly   Kate and the children send you there love and best Respects

and are wanting you to come down as they want to see you very
bad   your friends sends there Respects to you

I shall bring this to a close hoping this will find you well in health if
not doing well   And I want to see you as soon as I can

No more at this time   Farewell from your Cousin

ALS   Dave Waldrop[3]

> The struggle to reconstruct families was no new labor for many for-
> mer slaves. Martin Lee, who had been sold away from his first wife
> and other relatives in Georgia, subsequently purchased the free-
> dom of his mother, himself, and his second wife. Emancipation
> enabled him to expand his efforts and extend them to more distant
> kin—not only children and grandchildren but siblings, nieces, and
> nephews. When a nephew's former owner refused to surrender the
> boy and instead had him bound under the state apprenticeship law,
> Lee sought the assistance of the head of the Freedmen's Bureau in
> Georgia.

Florence Ala   December 7[the] 1866

Dear sir   I take the pleashure of writing you A fue lins hoping that I
will not ofende you by doing so   I was raised in your state and was sold
from their when I was 31 years olde   left wife one childe Mother
Brothers and sisters   My wife died about 12 years agoe and ten years
agoe I Made money And went back and bought My olde Mother and she
lives with Me   Seven years agoe I Maried again and commence to by
Myself and wife for two thousande dollars and last Christemas I Made
the last pay Ment and I have made Some little Money this year and I
wish to get my Kinde All with me and I will take it as a Greate favor if
you will help me to get them by sending me a order to Carey with me to
the agent of Monroe walton County Georgia   I was out their last weeke

Work gang returning from the sugar field. (*Century*, Nov. 1887)

and Got My daughter And hear childern but I could not Get My Sisters
Son   She is live and well   there is a Man by the name of Sebe—
Burson that ust to one them and he will not let me or his Mother have
the boy   he says he has the boy bound to him and the law in our State
is that a childe cannot be bounde when the[y] have Mother father
brother sistter uncl or Aunt that can take care of them but I went to the
Agent and he says the boy has not ben bounde to him his county and if I
will Give him 25 dollars he will deliver the boy to me but I think that to
harde and I hope you will Sende me a order that I can cary to Mr Arnel
so I May be Able to Get him without that much Money   I would not
Minde paying him 5 dollars and I think that far [*fair*]   I live 3
hunderde and 25 Miles from Monroe Ande it will cost me 3 hunderde
dollars to Get them to Alabma   pleas anser this as soon as you get it
and pleas dont sende to Georgia untill I goe   it Might Make it against
me   anser this to me and I will let you know the time I will starte and I
can get their in 2 days   pleas do the best you can for Me and I remain
yours a Servent And will untill death

Martin. Lee[4]

ALS

The Civil War, which made it possible to reunite black families, was
also a source of their dispersion. At war's end, an elderly freedman
asked the secretary of war for information about a nephew, hoping
against hope that a grave bearing the young man's name was not
the last resting place of his kin.

Charles City County   Va   May 14th 1865.

Hon. Sir.   will you be so obligeing as to give me information of my
nephue Theodore Mason Colored Born in the City of Richmond, Va.   I
think he Enlisted in the Army about the time they were Commencing to

Enlist men for the Colored Troops.   if you can give me any information about him being into the Army now or was Ever into It you alway may call me your Debter   what makes me ask for this information is that ware I live there is some Colored Troops Buried and on one of the graves is marked Theodore Mason Colored Soldier wich makes me think it is my Nephue   if you can give me news that my Nephue still lives you will make this old Darkey Happy again   Hon Sir you must Excuse my materiel for writing as this is the gift of a Union Soldier*   my address Hon Sir Is Erasmus Booman Charles City County. Va [via] Wilson Landing   Hon Sir if you will condesent to contencs this from one in truble you will recive the Blessing of a aged man near the Dread Portales of the unseen future   Hon Sir I remain your obeident Servant

ALS   Erasmus Booman[5]

> For the African-American people, the Civil War was indeed a broth-
> ers' war—sometimes quite literally so, as black men joined the
> Union army in the company of their brothers, cousins, and other
> relatives. Sarah Brown asked the secretary of war to locate her
> husband and the kinsmen with whom he had enlisted.

Philad[a] [Pa.]   February 8th 1865

Honl Sir   I am in great trouble of mind about my husband   it is reported that he is dead   he has been gone over a year and I have not hear from him   his name is Samuel or Sandy Brown Co. C. 25th regiment U. S. Colored Troops Penn   he went with his brother and five cousins to list   they are all in same Co. and regiment   none of them

---

* The letter is written on lined blue paper.

have been heard from only reports that they were dead which causes their wifes great grief.   You will be doing charity by letting us know there whereabouts if alive so that we may write to them.   Their names are Samuel or Sandy Brown Co. C. 25th regt Daniel Brown. Asa Miller. Daniel Horsey. George Horsey. Samuel Horsey George H. Washington   they all belong to same C° and regiment, other [dide?]   We have not received a cent from them since they left   we are all bad off it would do us a great favor if you would give the information as soon as your time will permit   I am your obedient servant

Sarah Brown

care of Peter Kelly N° 511 South 6th Street[6]

ALS

> Unfulfilled kinship obligations worried black soldiers whose terms of service continued into the postwar period. Having done their duty, they were eager to return home to take up their familial responsibilities once again, responsibilities that extended, in the case of Elijah Reeves, to an aged grandmother and orphaned sisters. In order to meet these obligations, Reeves asked his home-state senator to help him obtain a discharge.

Clarksville, Texas,   Sept. 14/65.

Sir: As an inhabitant of the State of Michigan I have the honor to respectfully claim your attention, and more, as one who precipitated himself into the chasm which the perfidious leaders of rebellion inaugurated with the vain hope of severing this great Republic, and rearing a government based on Chattel Slavery, I am confident that you will use your influence, which your magnanimity always prompts you to do, when the alleviating the condition of humanity calls it forth.

Now that Rebellion has been effectually crushed and the authority of the Government not only tolerated but re-established in all the seceded States, I most respectfully request that you take into consideration the facts which will be laid before you by the person delivering this letter, and apply to the Honble. Secretary of War for my discharge from the service of the United States.

Having manfully performed all the arduous duties of a soldier which devolved upon me while the destiny of the Country was yet uncertain, under adverse circumstances, and painful disadvantages, and that peace has again brightened our sky, the pecuniary circumstances of an aged grand mother and several orphan sisters whose sole dependence is on my earnings, prompts me to solicit, with your influence, my honorable discharge. Be assured, Sir, that in condescending to bestow on me and my orphan sisters this favor, your names will ever be remembered and the prayers of those suffering children shall never cease to ascend the throne in your behalf. I am, most Respectfully, Your Obdt. Humble Servt.

ALS   Elijah Reeves.[7]

Seeing them as a source of cheap labor, former slaveholders and other white southerners also took an interest in orphaned black children. Compliant local officials, sometimes with the cooperation of the Freedmen's Bureau, bound orphans into terms of apprenticeship that were but poorly disguised evocations of the old order. Freedpeople challenged such apprenticeships, demanding the release of loved ones. Occasionally, they sought to turn the apprenticeship laws to their own purposes by using them to obtain legal custody of children to whom they were related by blood or marriage. The following applications to a district Freedmen's Bureau officer in Petersburg, Virginia, display the assumption of familial responsibility by relatives who were willing to provide for such children despite their own limited resources.

Amelia Co[*urt*]. Ho[*use*]. [*Va.*]   June 11th 1866.

M[r] Barnz,   I wish to have my Cousin Wilson bound to me that is staying at M[r] Jefferson[s]   I have a house for him and will take care of him and do all I can for him   my brother[s] Albert and How will do the same   the reason I wish to get him from M[r] J[s] is because he is not treated well and as he is my Cousin I think it my duty to see to him   I wish you would see to it as soon as you can as I dont wish him to stay there any longer

HLSr   Sallie Harris.[8]

Amelia Co[*urt*]. Ho[*use*]. [*Va.*]   June the 12th [*18*]66

Dear Sir   Charles Ganaway is Sevin years of age neither farther or mother alive & at this time has no permanant home   as I married his Sister I feel it my duty to take care of him & most respectfully ask that you bind the said Charles Ganerway to me & at the proper time he shall have all that he is entitle to   Respectfully

HLSr   Wister Miller[9]

> A local bureau agent forwarded the applications of Sallie Harris
> and Wister Miller to the district headquarters, adding his own eval-
> uation of their merits.

Amelia C[*ourt*]. H[*ouse*]. V[a]   June 12 /66

Sir   I have the honor to hrewith transmit two applications of *Cold* people to have orphant children bound to them.   They are no doubt as well able as any of the cold people to fulfill their obligation.   As to Mr Jefferson, he is the white mans representative on the freedmans court,

Letter from Sallie Harris to a Freedmen's Bureau agent. (See p. 237) and does the *cause* justice.   He has the name of a hard master, but I do not know of his being cruel.   He has whiped the boy Wilson & I learned that he made him take off his shirt.   I do not know whether this is so or not.   I propose to enquire into it.   I sent the boys there with the understanding that I would apprintice them if agreeable to him, against the protest of all their relations, thinking it would be a good home.   The boys belonged to a Mr Rowlett & he last winter demanded that I should feed them or take them away.   Mr Jefferson after numerous promises took the boy Willson.   I then found that I, Rowlett had misinformed me, and that Wilson had lived with an uncle ever since he was free; and that he had been careing for & sending him to school,   He thought hard of my taking him away.   I met him yesterday and he said the reason he had said nothing was that Mr Jefferson had sent him word when he got the boy that he (the uncle) should hold his tounge & the least he said about it the better.   There is a decided opposition to binding these children to cold people and I write these particulars to show you the real state of feeling and seek your advice in the matter.   My object is to get good homes for these children.   Wealth, power or influence does not make a good home always.   The question is, in the present state of affairs, and considering the conditions of the col^d people, are they in your opinion ready to undertake these obligations.   If they are and you direct, I will make the "Indentures" to these petitioners.   I have no doubt in my [*mind*] that they will do all they promise to do.   I am very respectfuly your ob^t ser^t

HLcSr   W. F. White[10]

The struggle over orphaned children revealed the depth of kinship obligations among the former slaves. Moved by a sense of familial responsibility, grandparents, uncles, aunts, and other relatives volunteered to take custody of children whose parents were dead or unable to care for them, particularly when the children would otherwise fall into the hands of their former owners. Obdurate Freedmen's Bureau agents often believed that such kin were interested only in the children's labor, but they could not escape the demands, however inconvenient, of relatives who saw apprenticeship as nothing but slavery with a new name.

Clinton La.   Jary 10" 1867

Hon Sir   I am the mother of a woman Dina who is now dead   My Daugter Dina had a child boy by the name Porter.   I am a Colored woman former slave of a M[r] Sandy Spears of the parish of East Feliciana La.   Said Porter is now about Eleven years of age.   M[r] Spears has had the little boy Porter bound over to him so I am told by the agent of the Freedmen in this parish   I was not informed of this fact untill after the matter of binding was consumated   I do not wish to wrongfully interfere with the arrangement of those who are endeavoring to properly control us black people   I feel confident they are doing the best they can for us and our present condition—but I am the Grand Mother of Porter—   his Father Andrew is now and has been for some time a soldier in the army of the U.S.   he is I am told some where in Califonia   I do not know only that he is not here to see to the interest of his child   I am not by any means satisfied with the present arrangement made for my Grand Child Porter.   M[r] Spears I have known for many years.   I will say nothing of his faults, but I have the means of educating my Grand Child of doing a good part by him.   his Uncle who has been lately discharged from the army of the U.S— *Umphrey cold* who now resides in this parish is fully able to assist me in maintaining my Grand-Child Porter   we want him   we do not think M[r] Spears a suitable person to control this boy   M[r] Spears is very old

A family near Augusta, Georgia.
(Hargrett Rare Book and Manuscript Library, University of Georgia)

and infirm   he is and has been for many years addicted to the use of
ardent spirits   this fact I do not like to mention but truth requires me
to speak   now is there no chance to get my little boy   the agent of
this place will not listen to me, and I am required to call on you or I
must let my Grand-Child go which greatly grieves me. will you be so
kind after my statement to write to Elizabeth Collins f[ree]. w[oman of].
c[olor]. Clinton La the Step mother of Porter and advise her what I shall
do to obtain my little Grand Child.   please answer this letter and you
will greatly oblige   Truly yours a poor old black woman

Cyntha NicKols

f[ree]. w[oman of]. c[olor].[11]

ALS

[Endorsement by Lt. James DeGrey, Freedmen's Bureau agent] Parish
East Feliciana La. Clinton La   January 29" 1867 . . . . Sandy
Spears is as stated Old.—but not infirm.   he is addicted to ardent
Spirits, but not more so than the most of men in the Parish.   The boy
Porter is ten (10) years of age.   he (Spears) raised him from a
child.   My belief is, the old lady wants the boy because he is now able to
do Some work.   The binding out of children Seems to the freedmen like
putting them back into Slavery—   In every case where I have bound out
children, thus far Some Grand Mother or fortieth cousin has come to
have them released—

> The responsibility freedpeople felt for the care of orphans extended
> beyond the reach of blood and affinity. While stationed in eastern
> Arkansas, where many of them had been slaves, soldiers of the
> 56th U.S. Colored Infantry expended both their money and their
> labor to construct an orphanage for black children. A letter from
> one of the regiment's officers confirmed arrangements by which an
> association of Indiana Quakers would operate the institution.

Helena Ark   June 11 1866.

Gentlemen: Your favor of the 14th of April 1866 in which you accept
the trust of taking charge of the Orphan asylum established in Philips
Co Ark. by subscription of the Officers and men of this Regiment has
been recieved and a copy furnished each soldier.   Under the energetic
Management of Your Agent and trusty lady, Mr & Mrs Clark, the
institution progresses finely and I have no doubt its beneficial results
will be seen and acknowledged soon even by its opponents.   The Amount
of work that has been done on the grounds by the Soldiers is immense,
from an allmost unbroken forrest it has been cleared fenced and a large
part of it planted, and four substantial buildings erected suitable for the
wants of the children and those who have the Care of them.   It is
contemplated to dedicate the Institution on the next 4th of July in a
public manner with proper exercises.   And in behalf of the Regiment I
extend herewith to you an invitation to be present if convenient   Very
Truly Yours

ALcS   S J Clark[12]

NOTES

INTRODUCTION

1. Testimony of J. B. Roudanez before the American Freedmen's Inquiry Commission, 9 Feb. 1864, *Wartime Genesis: Lower South*, pp. 521–25.

2. Hawkins Wilson to Chief of the Freedmen's Bureau, at Richmond, 11 May 1867, enclosing Hawkins Wilson to Sister Jane, [11 May 1867], Letters Received, ser. 3892, Bowling Green VA Asst. Supt., BRFAL [A-8254]. A bracketed number at the end of a citation is that document's file number in the collection of the Freedmen and Southern Society Project.

CHAPTER 1

1. John Boston to Mrs. Elizabeth Boston, 12 Jan. 1862, *Destruction of Slavery*, pp. 357–58.

2. Maj. Genl. Geo. B. McClellan to Hon. Edwin Stanton, 21 Jan. 1862, A-587 1862, Letters Received, ser. 12, Records of the Adjutant General's Office.

3. Affidavit of Grandison Briscoe, 6 Feb. 1864, *Destruction of Slavery*, p. 365.

4. Nathan mc kinney to Maj. Genl. Banks, 2 Feb. 1863, *Destruction of Slavery*, p. 242.

5. Greer W. Davis to Major General Curtis, 24 Feb. 1863, *Destruction of Slavery*, pp. 449–50.

6. Testimony of Capt. C. B. Wilder before the American Freedmen's Inquiry Commission, 9 May 1863, *Destruction of Slavery*, pp. 88–90.

7. Affidavit of Amy Moore, [14? Aug. 1865], *Destruction of Slavery*, p. 567. For legal papers regarding the arrest and sale of Moore and her family, see *Destruction of Slavery*, pp. 568–70.

8. Brig. General [Augustus L. Chetlain] to Lieut. Col. T. H. Harris, 12 Apr. 1864, *Destruction of Slavery*, pp. 316–17.

9. Maj. Gen. S. R. Curtis to General, 13 Mar. 1864, *Destruction of Slavery*, pp. 480–81.

10. Asst. Adjt. Genl. James H. Steger to Col. Geo. H. Hall, 29 Mar. 1864, *Wartime Genesis: Upper South*, p. 599.

11. Affidavit of Jim Heiskell, [30 Mar. 1864], *Destruction of Slavery*, pp. 320–22.

12. Statement of Mrs. Laura A. Moody, 25 May 1864, *Destruction of Slavery*, pp. 379–80.

13. *Destruction of Slavery*, pp. 380–81.

14. John Q. A. Dennis to Hon. Stan, 26 July 1864, *Destruction of Slavery*, p. 386.

15. Brig. Gen. Edwd. A. Wild to Brig. Gen. G. F. Shepley, 1 Sept. 1864, *Destruction of Slavery*, pp. 98–99.

16. 1st Sgt. Joseph J. Harris to Gen. Ullman, 27 Dec. 1864, *Black Military Experience*, pp. 691–92.

17. Capt. F. B. Clark to Lieut. E. T. Lamberton, 15 Nov. 1865, *Black Military Experience*, pp. 750–51.

18. Endorsement of Maj. Genl. John M. Palmer, 30 Nov. 1865, *Black Military Experience*, p. 751.

19. *Black Military Experience*, p. 751n.

CHAPTER 2

1. *Justice* to Major Genl. N. P. Banks, 3 Apr. 1863, *Wartime Genesis: Lower South*, pp. 432–33.

2. Surgeon James Bryan to Hon. E. M. Stanton, 27 July 1863, *Wartime Genesis: Lower South*, pp. 715–17.

3. Affidavits of Ruben Win and Henry White, 21 Nov. 1863, *Wartime Genesis: Lower South*, p. 474.

4. Lieut. Col. Aug's. G. Bennett to Captain Wm. L. M. Burger, 30 Nov. 1863, *Wartime Genesis: Lower South*, p. 274.

5. *Wartime Genesis: Lower South*, pp. 274–75n.

6. Testimony of Mrs. Louisa Jane Barker, [Jan.? 1864], *Wartime Genesis: Upper South*, pp. 311–12.

7. Jane Wallis to Prof. Woodburry, [10 Dec. 1863], *Black Military Experience*, p. 138.

8. Statement of John Banks, 2 Jan. 1864, *Black Military Experience*, pp. 139–40.

9. Ned Baxter et al. to Major Genl. Butler, Sept. 1864, *Wartime Genesis: Upper South*, pp. 202–3.

10. Lieut. Col. John Foley to Lieut. Col. T. Harris, 11 Jan. 1865, *Black Military Experience*, p. 719.

11. Capt. T. A. Walker to Capt. J. S. Lord, 24 Jan. 1865, *Black Military Experience*, pp. 719–20.

12. Lt. Col. Jos. R. Putnam to Brig. Gen. W. D. Whipple, 30 Jan. 1865, *Wartime Genesis: Upper South*, pp. 460–61.

CHAPTER 3

1. *Official Records*, ser. 2, vol. 5, p. 797.

2. Hannah Johnson to Hon. Mr. Lincoln, 31 July 1863, *Black Military Experience*, pp. 582–83.

3. Aaron Peterson to Hon. Edwin M. Stanton, 29 Oct. 1863, *Black Military Experience*, p. 374.

4. Hiram A. Peterson to Mr. Babcok, 24 Oct. [1863], *Black Military Experience*, pp. 374–75.

5. Rosanna Henson to Abraham Lincoln, 11 July 1864, *Black Military Experience*, p. 680.

6. Sergt. John F. Shorter et al. to the President of the United States, 16 July 1864, *Black Military Experience*, pp. 401–2.

7. *Black Military Experience*, p. 367.

8. Rachel Ann Wicker to Mr. President Andrew, 12 Sept. 1864, *Black Military Experience*, pp. 402–3.

9. George Rodgers et al. to Mr. President, [Aug.] 1864, *Black Military Experience*, pp. 680–81.

10. Mrs. John W. Wilson to Hon. E. M. Stanton, 27 May 1865, *Black Military Experience*, p. 682.

11. George G. Freeman to U.S. Chief Justice, 25 June 1865, *Black Military Experience*, p. 379.

CHAPTER 4

1. Martha to My Dear Husband [Richard Glover], 30 Dec. 1863, *Black Military Experience*, p. 244.

2. Ann to My Dear Husband [Andrew Valentine], 19 Jan. 1864, *Black Military Experience*, pp. 686–87.

3. 1st Lieut. William P. Deming to Brig. Genl. Pile, 1 Feb. 1864, *Black Military Experience*, pp. 242–43.

4. Capt. Hiram Cornell to Col. J. P. Sanderson, 28 Mar. 1864, *Black Military Experience*, p. 688.

5. *Black Military Experience*, p. 688n.

6. Col. John F. Tyler to Col. J. H. Baker, 12 Jan. 1865, *Wartime Genesis: Upper South*, pp. 612–13.

7. Affidavit of Patsey Leach, 25 Mar. 1865, *Black Military Experience*, pp. 268–69.

8. Affidavit of John Burnside, 15 Dec. 1864, *Wartime Genesis: Upper South*, pp. 687–88.

9. Affidavit of Abisha Scofield, 16 Dec. 1864, *Black Military Experience*, pp. 715–16.

10. Lieut. Col. D. M. Sells to Capt. F. W. Draper, 6 Feb. 1865, *Destruction of Slavery*, p. 613.

11. Affidavit of Frances Johnson, 25 Mar. 1865, *Black Military Experience*, pp. 694–95.

12. *Statutes at Large*, vol. 13, p. 571.

13. Affidavit of William Jones, 29 Mar. 1865, *Black Military Experience*, p. 276.

14. H. G. Mosee to Secratary Stanton, 1 Apr. 1865, *Black Military Experience*, p. 696.

15. For the proclamation of December 18, 1865, announcing the ratification of the Thirteenth Amendment, see *Statutes at Large*, vol. 13, pp. 774–75.

16. jane coward to Dear Husband, [6] July 1865, *Black Military Experience*, p. 697.

CHAPTER 5

1. Major General E. O. C. Ord to Brig. Genl. George H. Gordon, 12 May 1865, *Black Military Experience*, pp. 721–22.

2. Chaplain Wm. A. Green et al. to Maj. Genl. O. O. Howard, 5 June 1865, *Black Military Experience*, pp. 727–28.

3. Sergt. Richard Etheredge and Wm. Benson to Genl. Howard, [May or June 1865], *Black Military Experience*, pp. 729–30.

4. Brevet Brig. General Geo. W. Cole to [25th Army Corps Headquarters], [June 1865], *Black Military Experience*, pp. 723–24.

5. Unsigned to Sir, Dec. 1865, *Black Military Experience*, pp. 725–27.

6. Emily Waters to My Dear Husband, 16 July 1865, *Black Military Experience*, p. 698.

7. Alsie Thomas to My Dear Brother, 30 July 1865, *Black Military Experience*, p. 699.

8. 2nd Lieut. Hugh P. Beach to Mr. Thomas W. Conway, 1 Aug. 1865, *Black Military Experience*, pp. 699–700.

9. [Etta Waters] to My Dear Husband, 26 July [1865], *Black Military Experience*, p. 668.

10. Unsigned to Mr. E. M. Stanton, 22 Oct. 1865, A-420 1865, *Black Military Experience*, pp. 425–26.

11. Unsigned to General Sickels, 13 Jan. 1866, *Black Military Experience*, pp. 777–78.

12. Norman Riley to Dear wife, 12 Aug. 1865, *Black Military Experience*, p. 703.

13. Norman Riley to Dear wife, 26 Aug. 1865, *Black Military Experience*, pp. 703–4.

14. Catherine Riley to Norman Riley, 28 Aug. 1865, *Black Military Experience*, pp. 704–5.

15. Norman Riley to Dear wife, 22 Sept. 1865, *Black Military Experience*, p. 705.

16. W. G. Bond to Brvt. Lieut. Col. J. H. Cochrane, 19 Dec. 1865, *Black Military Experience*, pp. 705–6.

17. *Black Military Experience*, p. 706n.

18. Affidavit of Catherine Riley, 5 May 1866, *Black Military Experience*, pp. 706–7.

19. Endorsement of Joshua Cobb, 24 May 1866, on ibid., *Black Military Experience*, pp. 707–8.

20. James Herney to Seceretary Stanten, 15 May 1866, *Black Military Experience*, pp. 778–79.

21. Capt. G. E. Stanford et al. to Mr. President and the Ceterry of War, 30 May 1866, *Black Military Experience*, pp. 779–81.

CHAPTER 6

1. Chaplain John Eaton, Jr., to Lt. Col. Jno. A. Rawlins, 29 Apr. 1863, *Wartime Genesis: Lower South*, pp. 684–97. Interrogatory numbers and italicized place names appearing in the margin of the manuscript have been inserted into the body of the text.

2. Vicksburg marriage register, vol. 43, pp. 386–87, *Black Military Experience*, pp. 710–11.

3. Private Aaron Oats to Hon. Ed. M. Stanton, 26 Jan. 1865, *Black Military Experience*, pp. 692–93.

4. Lucrethia to Dar husban [Aaron Oats], 22 Dec. 1864, *Black Military Experience*, p. 693.

5. [Jerry Smith] to Aaron Utz, 10 Jan. 1865, *Black Military Experience*, pp. 693–94.

6. Chaplain A. B. Randall to Brig. Gen. L. Thomas, 28 Feb. 1865, *Black Military Experience*, p. 712.

7. Marriage certificate of Rufus Wright and Elisabeth Turner, 3 Dec. 1863, *Black Military Experience*, p. 662.

8. Rufus Wright to Dear wife, 2[2] Apr. 1864, *Black Military Experience*, p. 661.

9. Ruphus Wright to dear wife, 25 May 1864, *Black Military Experience*, p. 663.

10. Affidavit of Elisabeth Wright, 21 Aug. 1865, *Black Military Experience*, pp. 663–64.

11. J. R. Johnson to Col. S. P. Lee, 1 June 1866, *Black Military Experience*, p. 672.

12. 1st Lt. F. E. Grossmann to the Actg. Asst. Adjt. General, 1 Oct. 1866, G-41 1866, Letters Received, ser. 586, FL Asst. Commissioner, BRFAL [A-1102].

13. J. H. Lyman to Bv. Capt. F. E. Grossman, 3 Oct. 1866, vol. 5, p. 8, Letters Sent, ser. 582, FL Asst. Commissioner, BRFAL [A-1102]. On the reinterpretation of child-custody law in the nineteenth century, see Michael Grossberg, *Governing the Hearth: Law and the Family in Nineteenth-Century America* (Chapel Hill, N.C., 1985), pp. 234–53.

14. J. E. Eldredge to Agt. Freedmans Bureau Willmingto N.C., 29 July 1867, Letters Received, ser. 2892,

Wilmington NC Subasst. Commissioner, BRFAL [A-806].

15. Willie Ann Grey to Philip Grey, 7 Apr. 1866, Registered Letters Received, ser. 4239, Richmond VA Supt. 3rd District, BRFAL [A-8154].

16. Statement of John Berry, 11 Aug. 1865, *Black Military Experience*, p. 799.

17. Affidavit of Rosa Freeman, 24 July 1866, Affidavits & Papers Relating to Complaints, ser. 1017, Savannah GA Subasst. Commissioner, BRFAL [A-5781].

18. Mrs. Catherine Massey to Hon. Edwin M. Stanton, 10 July 1865, *Black Military Experience*, pp. 667–68.

19. Affidavit of Sarah Fields, 6 July 1866, *Black Military Experience*, pp. 673–74.

20. Affidavit of Jackson Field, 6 July 1866, *Black Military Experience*, p. 674.

21. Affidavit of Susan Taylor, 7 July 1866, *Black Military Experience*, pp. 674–75.

22. *Black Military Experience*, p. 675n.

23. Capt. M. Mitchell to Major [A. T. Reeve], 20 Dec. 1865, *Black Military Experience*, p. 671.

24. M. C. Fulton to Brig. Genl. Davis Tilson, 17 Apr. 1866, Unregistered Letters Received, ser. 632, GA Asst. Commissioner, BRFAL [A-5379].

25. "I am Committee," n.d., enclosed in Lt. Chas. B. Brady to Bvt. Lt. Col. A. L. Hough, 29 Jan. 1867, B-10 1867, Letters Received, ser. 4720, Dept. of the Tennessee, U.S. Army Continental Commands [C-2027].

26. Case of S. G. Wilson v. Jackson Irving, 2 Sept. 1867, vol. 169, pp. 52–53, Register of Complaints, ser. 2203,

Jackson MS Subasst. Commissioner, BRFAL [A-9365]. The witnesses' names, which appear in the left-hand margin of the complaint register, have been incorporated into the text.

CHAPTER 7

1. [Private Spotswood Rice] to My Children, [3 Sept. 1864], *Black Military Experience*, p. 689.

2. Spotswood Rice to Kittey diggs, [3 Sept. 1864], *Black Military Experience*, p. 690.

3. George Washington to Mr. Abrham Lincoln, 4 Dec. 1864, *Destruction of Slavery*, p. 608.

4. Affidavit of Joseph Miller, 26 Nov. 1864, *Black Military Experience*, pp. 269–71.

5. *Wartime Genesis: Upper South*, pp. 680–93.

6. Affidavit of Minta Smith, 3 Apr. 1867, *Black Military Experience*, pp. 676–77.

7. Harison smith to my dear sister, 9 Mar. 1867, *Black Military Experience*, pp. 677–78.

8. Affidavit of Harriet Ann Bridwell, 3 Apr. 1867, *Black Military Experience*, pp. 678–79.

9. *Black Military Experience*, pp. 678–79.

10. Proceedings in Louisville Freedmen's Bureau Court, 28 May [1867], *Black Military Experience*, p. 679.

11. [Jane Welcome] to abarham lincon, 21 Nov. 1864, *Black Military Experience*, p. 664.

12. *Black Military Experience*, p. 665n.

13. Richard Henry Tebout to My kind friend, 26 Sept. 1865, *Black Military Experience*, p. 669.

14. *Black Military Experience*, p. 670n.

15. G. H. Freeman to Madam, 19 Aug. 1864, *Black Military Experience*, pp. 600–601.

16. Martha Wells to Assistant Adjutant Genl. T. W. Taggard, 24 Dec. 1866, *Black Military Experience*, pp. 675–76.

17. Capt. Andrew Stafford to General H. H. Lockwood, 4 Nov. 1864, *Wartime Genesis: Upper South*, pp. 510–11.

18. Statement of Jane Kamper, 14 Nov. 1864, *Wartime Genesis: Upper South*, p. 519.

19. Milly Johnson to Sir, 26 Mar. 1867, Letters Received, ser. 2686, Hillsboro NC Asst. Subasst. Commissioner, BRFAL [A-983].

20. Affidavit of Rebecca Parsons, 28 Apr. 1867, P-383 1867, Letters Received, ser. 631, GA Asst. Commissioner, BRFAL [A-117].

21. Chaplain L. S. Livermore to Lt. Col. R. S. Donaldson, 10 Jan. 1866, "L" 1866, Registered Letters Received, ser. 2188, Jackson MS Acting Asst. Commissioner of the Northern District of Mississippi, BRFAL [A-9328].

22. Affidavit of Enoch Braston, 10 Jan. 1866, enclosed in ibid.

23. Joe Bright to Worthy Cornell, 26 Apr. 1866, Letters Received, ser. 2892, Wilmington NC Supt. of the Southern Dist., BRFAL [A-783].

CHAPTER 8

1. Annie Davis to Mr. president, 25 Aug. 1864, *Destruction of Slavery*, p. 384.

2. Affidavit of Adam Woods, 11 Nov. 1867, #569 1867, Letters Received, ser. 1208, Louisville KY Subasst. Commissioner, BRFAL [A-4513].

3. Dave Waldrop to Sarah Jones, 18 June 1867, enclosed in Lieut. L. J. Whiting to Col. O. D. Kinsman, 2 July 1867,

Unregistered Letters Received, ser. 9, AL Asst. Commissioner, BRFAL [A-1903]. The cover letter requested government transportation for "Mrs. Sarah Jones and three (3) children from Montgomery, Alabama, to Milton, Florida."

4. Martin Lee to Mr. Tillson, 7 Dec. 1866, Unregistered Letters Received, ser. 632, GA Asst. Commissioner, BRFAL [A-5416].

5. Erasmus Booman to Hon. Edward M. Stanton, 14 May 1865, *Black Military Experience*, pp. 666–67.

6. Sarah Brown to Honl. E. M. Stanton, 8 Feb. 1865, *Black Military Experience*, p. 665.

7. Musician Elijah Reeves to Honble. Z. Chandler, 14 Sept. 1865, *Black Military Experience*, pp. 774–75.

8. Sallie Harris to Mr. Barnz, 11 June 1866, Letters & Orders Received, ser. 3881, Amelia Courthouse VA Asst. Supt., BRFAL [A-8116].

9. Wister Miller to Capt. Barns, 12 June 1866, Letters & Orders Received, ser. 3881, Amelia Courthouse VA Asst. Supt., BRFAL [A-8116].

10. Capt. W. F. White to Capt. Stuart Barnes, 12 June 1866, vol. 102, pp. 150–51, Letters Sent, ser. 3879, Amelia Courthouse VA Asst. Supt., BRFAL [A-8116].

11. Cyntha Nickols to the chief Agent of the Freedmen Bureau at N.O. La., 10 Jan. 1867, N-1 1867, Letters Received, ser. 1303, LA Asst. Commissioner, BRFAL [A-8620].

12. 1st Lieut. S. J. Clark to Joseph Dickenson and Timothy Harrison, 11 June 1866, *Black Military Experience*, p. 763.

INDEX